# La-5
## vs
# Fw 190

## Eastern Front 1942–45

# DMITRIY KHAZANOV & ALEKSANDER MEDVED

First published in Great Britain in 2011 by Osprey Publishing,
Midland House, West Way, Botley, Oxford, OX2 0PH, UK
44–02 23rd St, Suite 219, Long Island City, NY 11101, USA
E-mail: info@ospreypublishing.com
OSPREY PUBLISHING IS PART OF THE OSPREY GROUP

A CIP catalogue record for this book is available from the British
Library.

Print ISBN: 978 1 84908 473 4
PDF e-book ISBN: 978 1 84908 474 1
EPUB e-book ISBN: 978 1 84908 873 2

Edited by Tony Holmes
Cover artwork and battlescene by Gareth Hector
Three-views by Andrey Yurgenson
Cockpit, gunsight and armament scrap artwork by Jim Laurier
Page layout by Ken Vail Graphic Design, Cambridge, UK
Index by Alan Thatcher
Typeset in Adobe Garamond
Maps by Bounford.com
Originated by PDQ Digital Media Solutions
Printed in China through Bookbuilders

11 12 13 14 15    10 9 8 7 6 5 4 3 2 1

Osprey Publishing is supporting the Woodland Trust, the UK's leading
woodland conservation charity, by funding the dedication of trees.

## Editor's note

For ease of comparison please refer to the following conversion table:

1 mile = 1.6km
1lb = 0.45kg
1yd = 0.9m
1ft = 0.3m
1in = 2.54cm/25.4mm
1 gallon = 4.5 litres

## La-7 cover art

On 22 March 1945, as the Red Army battled its way through to Berlin, the
ranking Soviet ace Major Ivan Kozhedub of 176th GIAP (Guards Fighter Aviation
Regiment) engaged a formation of eight Fw 190s near the Seelow Heights – soon
to be the site of one of the bloodiest battles of World War II. Despite the uneven
odds, Kozhedub and his wingman, Dmitriy Nechaev, were confident that their
La-7s would prevail. 'I spotted the eight-aircraft formation of Focke-Wulfs
approaching us from behind', explained Kozhedub. 'I had no time to think. The
fighters were below us, forming an arc in the air. I was flying at quite a high speed,
so I climbed sharply and banked my fighter to the right in a tight wingover turn.
The lead Fw 190 pilot also climbed and turned to the right in my direction,
having seen that I was preparing to defend myself from their attack. His
manoeuvre had an obvious goal – to gain an advantage in altitude and, after
assessing the situation, to attack Nechaev and I. However, at this moment the
Fw 190s split up, lacking combat coordination and support, so I took advantage
of this. Sharply turning defence into attack, I fell like a rock on the last fighter in
the formation. With Nechaev covering me, I fired at point blank range and the
Focke-Wulf burst into flames and dived into the ground. I then took a look
around and spotted the leader of the German fighters – which were now above
us – trying to close onto our tails. Making the most of the La-7's excellent rate
of turn, I managed to get in behind him and, while still inverted, took aim and
opened fire. The long burst hit the fighter, and pieces flew off it as the Fw 190 fell
away and crashed. I had just scored my 60th victory'. (Artwork by Gareth Hector)

## Fw 190 cover art

The leading German ace in terms of La-5/7 victories was the legendary Walter
Nowotny, who claimed at least 49 Lavochkin fighters destroyed between 7 March
and 14 October 1943. The first pilot in history to achieve 250 aerial victories,
Nowotny routinely downed multiple La-5s in single missions during the course
of 1943 while flying Fw 190A-5/6s with I./JG 54. In this particular action on
14 September, he claimed two La-5s from 286th IAD (Fighter Aviation Division)
at low altitude while defending I./JG 54's airfield at Shatalovka-East, on the Kursk
front. The base was repeatedly attacked by Soviet Il-2 and Pe-2 bombers for 48
hours, and during this period Nowotny claimed 14 kills – five of them escorting
La-5s. The Lavochkins seen being downed in this specially commissioned artwork
were the ace's 206th and 207th victories. By the time Nowotny left the Eastern
Front in November 1943, his overall tally stood at 255 kills. (Gareth Hector)

| German rank | Soviet equivalent |
|---|---|
| Reichsmarschall | Chief Marshal for Aviation (*Glavny Marshal Aviatsii*) |
| Generalfeldmarschall | Marshal for Aviation (*Marshal Aviatsii*) |
| Generaloberst | Colonel General (*General Polkovnik*) |
| General der Flieger | no equivalent |
| Generalleutnant | Lieutenant General (*General Leytenant*) |
| Generalmajor | Major General (*General Mayor*) |
| Oberst | Colonel (*Polkovnik*) |
| Oberstleutnant | Lieutenant Colonel (*Podpolkovnik*) |
| Major | Major (*Mayor*) |
| Hauptmann | Captain (*Kapitan*) |
| Oberleutnant | Senior Lieutenant (*Starshiy Leytenant*) |
| Leutnant | Lieutenant (*Leytenant*) |
| Stabsfeldwebel | no equivalent |
| Oberfähnrich | no equivalent |
| Oberfeldwebel | Master Sergeant (*Starshina*) |
| Fähnrich | no equivalent |
| Feldwebel | Sergeant (*Serjant*) |
| Unteroffizier | Junior Sergeant (*Mladshiy Serjant*) |
| Hauptgefreiter | no equivalent |
| Obergefreiter | no equivalent |
| Gefreiter | Corporal (*Efreytor*) |
| Flieger | Red Army man (*Krasnoarmeets*) |

# CONTENTS

# INTRODUCTION

Soviet aeronautical engineers and pilots from the Red Army Air Force (*Voenno-Vozdushniye Sily Krasnoy Armii*, abbreviated to VVS-KA) were able to familiarise themselves with German military aircraft long before the invasion of the USSR in June 1941. Some had been captured in Spain during the Civil War and sent back to the Soviet Union, while others were bought from the Germans following the signing of the infamous non-aggression pact between the two countries in August 1939.

Having studied the Luftwaffe's principal fighter, the Messerschmitt Bf 109E, and compared its flight data with the then new MiG-3, Yak-1 and LaGG-3, both the leadership of the VVS-KA and senior aircraft designers came to the conclusion in early 1941 that Soviet fighters had at last attained parity with their western European equivalents.

However, in the immediate aftermath of the launching of Operation *Barbarossa* on 22 June 1941, it quickly became apparent that the E-model's replacement, the Bf 109F, was clearly superior to all Russian fighters then in frontline service. For example, the 'Friedrich' was faster than all three new Soviet fighters up to an altitude of 16,500ft – fighting rarely occurred at higher altitudes on the Eastern Front.

The Bf 109F's resulting mastery of the skies greatly assisted the Wehrmacht in its advance into the USSR. Indeed, German troops had progressed so far east by the autumn and winter of 1942 that the Soviet aviation industry had to endure a painful, but necessary, evacuation to the country's eastern regions. Such a move further hindered the development of a homegrown fighter with the performance to rival the Bf 109F at just the time when frontline units in the VVS-KA were crying out for such a machine. Fortunately, the harsh Soviet winters of 1941 and 1942 did what Russian forces could not, stopping the German advance short of Moscow and allowing the Red Army to launch a series of counteroffensives in the south of the country.

Despite some success on the ground, VVS-KA units were still struggling to field a fighter that could match the Bf 109F. However, leading fighter designer Semyon Alekseyevich Lavochkin and his team of engineers had commenced work the previous year on a radial-engined version of his LaGG-3, the latter machine's 1,240hp Klimov M-105PF inline engine being replaced by an air-cooled Shvetsov M-82 radial of 1,700hp. Initially christened the LaG-5, the prototype proved to be some 37mph faster than the LaGG-3 in early flight testing, and it also boasted a superior rate of climb and better horizontal manoeuvrability, although its agility in the vertical plane was somewhat diminished. The new fighter was hastily rushed into production in Molotov (Perm).

By the time the first examples reached frontline units in August 1942, the LaG-5 had been redesignated the Lavochkin La-5. That same month saw the service debut of the re-engined Bf 109G-2, fitted with a more powerful Daimler-Benz DB 605. Perhaps more importantly, on 6 September I./JG 51 arrived on the Eastern Front with the first examples of an all new fighter type that would rival the La-5 for aerial supremacy – the Focke-Wulf Fw 190A. Like its Soviet rival, the Focke-Wulf was powered by an air-cooled radial engine of much the same horsepower in the form of the BMW 801. The new fighter was both fast and highly manoeuvrable, and was at its best at medium to low altitudes.

In an effort to retain parity with the Bf 109G and Fw 190A, Lavochkin improved the reliability and performance of the Shvetsov engine, initially with the introduction of the M-82F, which gave the resulting La-5F better performance at lower altitudes thanks to its unlimited boost. Just as this variant entered service in late 1942, Lavochkin commenced flight-testing the definitive M-82FN-engined La-5FN. With direct fuel injection, the new motor was ten per cent more powerful than the standard M-82. And with most of the early structural and mechanical defects that plagued the La-5 now eradicated, the La-5FN could rival – and in some instances better – the performance of the Bf 109G-6 and Fw 190A-5 by the summer of 1943.

Although the Focke-Wulf would remain a significant threat to the VVS-KA into early 1944, by then Soviet pilots had come to realise that most of the fighter units equipped with the Fw 190 had been posted back to Germany to defend its cities against daylight bomber raids being mounted by the USAAF's Eighth and Fifteenth Air Forces. Indeed, by the spring of 1944 most Fw 190-equipped *Gruppen* on the Eastern Front were *Schlacht* (ground attack) units. These machines were not flown by *Experten* who had amassed vast experience engaging Soviet fighters, but by ex-Ju 87 and Hs 129 pilots with only limited knowledge of aerial combat. The Focke-Wulf gradually became a less dangerous foe for Soviet fighter pilots as a result, although the Bf 109G/K remained a threat through to war's end.

The VVS-KA enjoyed even greater supremacy in the air from the autumn of 1944 following the introduction of the La-7. Flight-testing of the new Lavochkin fighter at the VVS NII KA (Red Army Air Force Scientific Research Institute) showed that its performance was superior to any version of the Bf 109 or Fw 190 fielded by the Luftwaffe at the altitudes at which combat occurred on the Eastern Front. Indeed, it could be claimed that the La-7 was the best Soviet fighter in series production in May 1945.

Pilots from 159th IAP conduct a preflight briefing in front of an La-5, complete with a rousing inscription, on the Leningrad front in the spring of 1943. Note the absence of the distinctive 'F' marking on the fighter's engine cowling, which means that the aircraft was powered by an early version of the M-82 engine.

# CHRONOLOGY

## 1937
**September**  *Reichsluftfahrtministerium* (RLM) places a development contract with Focke-Wulf Flugzeugbau GmbH for a single-seat interceptor fighter to supplement the Messerschmitt Bf 109. Work on the project begins late in 1937 under the direction of Diplom-Ingenieur Kurt Tank.

## 1938
**18 July**  Focke-Wulf issues the drawings for the first prototype Fw 190 (V1).

## 1939
**1 June**  Hans Sander performs the Fw 190 V1's maiden flight from Bremen.

**29 July**  The development of an all-wooden fighter powered by a Klimov M-105 inline engine is entrusted to designers V. P. Gorbunov, S. A. Lavochkin and M. I. Gudkov (who form the LaGG design bureau) via a decree issued by the Soviet government.

## 1940
**January**  Focke-Wulf and BMW commence development work on the BMW 801 radial engine for the Fw 190 as a replacement for the BMW 139 powerplant.

**30 March**  I-301 prototype makes its first flight, with A. I. Nikashin at the controls.

**December**  Soviet government decree orders the I-301 into series production as the LaGG-1. Not a single example is built, however, as the increased range LaGG-3 is given priority. Boasting improved fuel capacity and armament, as well as an uprated M-105P engine, the LaGG-3 is soon being built in five plants.

A fantastic view inside an assembly hall at Focke-Wulf's Bremen plant. The Fw 190 was a well-designed aeroplane, with good access to most of its major systems and equipment. Focke-Wulf provided excellent access to the aircraft's BMW 801 engine, incorporating large cowling panels into the design which, if necessary, could be removed altogether for maintenance.

## 1941
**May**  Fw 190A-1 series production commences.

## 1942
**March**  LaGG-3 fitted with a Shvetsov M-82 radial makes its first flight.

**May**  Series production of the M-82-powered LaG-5, as the new aircraft is designated (then abbreviated to La-5 in September), commences at Factory No. 21 in Gorkiy.

**August**  First LaG-5s to reach the frontline are issued to 49th IAP, and these make their combat debut on 14 August near Beliy. The unit claims 16 enemy aircraft downed in its first 17 missions for the loss of ten LaG-5s.

**6 September**  I./JG 51 arrives back at Lyuban, southeast of Leningrad, after taking just two weeks to transition from the Bf 109F to the Fw 190A-3.

**29 September**   Hauptmann Heinrich Krafft, *gruppenkommandeur* of I./JG 51, claims an I-16 as the Fw 190's first victory on the Eastern Front.

## 1943

**January**   I./JG 54 flies in to Krasnogvardeisk, on the Leningrad front, having re-equipped with Fw 190A-4s. JGs 51 and 54 have around 140 Focke-Wulfs on strength between them by month-end.

**8 February**   La-5 pilot Lt P. A. Grazhdaninov of 210th IAD's 169th IAP is credited with downing the first Fw 190 to fall in Soviet-held territory.

**March**   Fw 190G ground attack variant enters service on the Eastern Front with *Schlachtgeschwader* 1, and the type plays a key role in the tank battle of Kursk in early July.

**March**   First examples of the La-5F, fitted with M-82F 'boosted' engine, reach frontline units from Factory No. 21 in Gorkiy.

**July**   First series-production standard La-5FNs reach 32nd GIAP just in time to participate in the Battle of Kursk. During the latter the regiment's pilots fly 25 missions and bring down 33 German aircraft, including 21 Fw 190s, for the loss of six La-5FNs.

**22 August**   Future ranking Soviet ace I. N. Kozhedub of 240th IAP destroys his first Fw 190, taking his tally to nine overall.

**14 October**   Hauptmann Walter Nowotny of I./JG 54 claims six victories (two of which are La-5s) to become the first fighter pilot to achieve 250 kills.

**3 November**   Leutnant Emil 'Bully' Lang of 5./JG 54 claims a staggering 17 victories (including three La-5s) during the course of four missions around Kiev.

## 1944

**1 February**   La-7 prototype successfully completes its first flight, and the aircraft soon passes flight-testing and is cleared for series production.

**September**   63rd GIAP gives the La-7 its combat debut, 30 aircraft being assigned to the regiment on the 1st Baltic Front. 462 sorties are flown during one month and 55 enemy aircraft shot down for the loss of eight La-7s.

## 1945

**1 January**   Of the 1,331 ground attack aircraft at the Luftwaffe's disposal, 1,077 are Fw 190Fs.

**14 February**   Oberleutnant Otto Kittel of I./JG 54 is killed attacking an Il-2. He claimed 267 victories (including 30 La-5s) with the Fw 190, making him the type's most successful pilot.

**17 April**   Maj Ivan Kozhedub, now serving with La-7-equipped 176th GIAP, downs two Fw 190s over Berlin to take his final tally to 62 victories. At least 14 of these were Fw 190s, 11 of them being claimed between 10 February and 17 April 1945.

An airframe checklist is consulted by a foreman and an assembly line worker in Factory No. 21 at Gorkiy in late 1944 as near-complete La-7s are prepared for roll-out following construction. Factories No. 99 in Ulan-Ude and No. 391 in Moscow also built La-7s.

# DESIGN AND DEVELOPMENT

## La-5 and La-7

On 29 July 1939 a small team of designers under the leadership of Vladimir Gorbunov received instructions via a decree from the Soviet government to design and manufacture a fast, all-wooden fighter that was to be designated the I-301. Two days later, Gorbunov and his engineering colleagues Semyon Lavochkin and Mikhail Gudkov were sent by order of the People's Commissariat for the Aviation Industry (NKAP) to small aircraft plant No. 301, which had been specially established as an experimental and production base for the group. This site had previously housed a factory making furniture for the Palace of the Soviets.

Gorbunov was placed in overall charge of the fighter project, Lavochkin was responsible for the aircraft's design and durability and Gudkov oversaw the supply of raw materials and manufacturing. The new design bureau was christened LaGG, the name being derived from the initials of its principal engineers. Shortly after the company had been formed, the NKAP leadership replaced Gorbunov with Lavochkin, officially making him the Chief Designer of the I-301.

On 30 March 1940, test pilot Aleksey Nikashin took to the skies for the first time in the new machine. Unlike rival designs from MiG and Yakovlev, which featured conventional mixed construction, LaGG's fighter was built from a special plywood known as delta-drevsina, which had been impregnated with phenols derived from birch tars. The latter allowed the plywood to be moulded into various aerodynamic shapes, and although heavier than conventional wood, it was also stronger and fire resistant. This material had been specifically chosen by LaGG due to its ease of manufacture and reliance on a natural resource that the Soviet Union had a limitless supply of – trees. By contrast, the USSR could only secure duralumin in modest quantities in 1940, thus slowing production of rival designs from Yakovlev and MiG.

Once built, the streamlined I-301 received a coat of deep cherry red varnish that earned it the nickname 'the piano' because of its colour. Powered by a Klimov M-105P engine, the unarmed prototype achieved a top speed of 376mph in level during one of its early test flights. This impressive performance was systematically eroded in coming months as the VVS-KA asked for various modifications to the aircraft that made it increasingly heavy. On 2 October 1940 LaGG was told that the fighter's range had to be doubled to 621 miles, so additional fuel tanks were fitted in the wings between the spars. The I-301's nose-mounted armament of a single MP-6 23mm cannon and two Berezin UB 12.7mm machine guns was also installed, as was other basic operational equipment such as seat armour and radio receivers.

By 1 December 1940, when the I-301 was renamed the LaGG-1 (from then on fighters in Soviet service were designated with odd numbers and aircraft of other purpose even numbers), the fighter's top speed had dropped to 357mph and its rate of climb had also been reduced. Not a single LaGG-1 was built, however, as all plants had been prepared for construction of the improved LaGG-3 – the Soviet government had ordered that 805 examples were to be delivered to frontline units by 1 July 1941. Five aircraft plants were chosen to fulfill this request, namely No. 21 at Gorkiy (today's Nizhniy Novgorod), No. 23 in Leningrad (now St Petersburg), No. 31 in Taganrog, No. 153 in Novosibirsk and No. 463 in Tallinn. Chief Designer Lavochkin was sent to Gorkiy to oversee production while Vladimir Gorbunov travelled to Taganrog.

The first production LaGG-3s were completed in December 1940 at Plant No. 23, and once examples started to reach operational units several months later they began to suffer from engine overheating, radiator and hydraulic system leakages and the breaking of connecting rods due to heavy ailerons and elevators. The general build quality of the aircraft also left much to be desired, with rags left in pipelines, tools forgotten in the airframe, nuts and bolts left loose and parts fitted carelessly. Finally, the cockpit transparency, made of a nitro-cellulose compound, also drew heavy criticism for its poor visibility and rapid yellowing when exposed to sunlight.

Things only got worse for LaGG-3 units following the German invasion of the Soviet Union on 22 June 1941, for the fighter's now-poor performance was cruelly exposed. With its top speed reduced to 332mph at best, plagued by poor handling characteristics, sluggish controls and an inadequate rate of turn, the 322 LaGG-3s that had reached the frontline by June were 'easy meat' for the swarms of Bf 109E/Fs that hunted down VVS-KA fighters during Operation *Barbarossa*. These problems were further exacerbated by poor leadership in Soviet fighter regiments, outdated tactics and a general lack of familiarity with new types such as the LaGG-3. Surviving pilots in the frontline whispered amongst themselves that the type designation LaGG stood for '*Lakirovannyi, Garantirovannyi Grob*', which translates into 'Guaranteed, Lacquered Coffin'.

Early combat reports detailing its poor showing provoked stinging criticism from Premier Joseph Stalin himself, and the leadership of VVS-KA bluntly stated that the LaGG-3 was seriously inferior to the Yak-1 fighter in terms of its speed,

La-5/7 designer Semyon Alekseevich Lavochkin is seen at work. During the war years all Soviet aircraft designers were given both military ranks and uniforms. Made a Hero of Socialist Labour, Lavochkin played an active role in the development of Soviet first generation jet fighters post-war before his Scientific Production Organisation was given the task of developing anti-aircraft rockets. In the summer of 1960 he suffered a heart attack at a test range in Central Asia and passed away a short while later.

LaGG-3 Series 29 'Red 59' force-landed in a bog on the Leningrad Front in early 1942 and was subsequently retrieved by 3rd GIAP-KBF. Returned to airworthiness, it was flown by ace Igor Kaberov for several weeks in February 1942 until damaged once again and sent back to a repair depot. Kaberov's regiment transitioned from LaGG-3s to La-5s in late 1942, and the ace ended the war with 28 victories to his name.

OPPOSITE
This La-7 was flown by Maj Vladimir Lavrinenkov, Regimental Commander of 9th GIAP, from several airfields in East Prussia during the final months of the war. Maj Lavrinenkov used '17' as his personal number throughout the war (he was born on 17 May 1919), whilst the lightning bolt marking on either side of the fuselage was similar to the symbol applied by the French-manned *Normandie-Niemen* Regiment to its Yaks. Both units served in the same division. By May 1945 Lavrinenkov had flown 448 missions, fought in 134 aerial battles and claimed 36 individual and 11 shared kills.

manoeuvrability and ease of flying. Nevertheless, the LaGG-3 remained in production because unlike the Yak-1, it was easy to build due to an abundance of raw materials.

Stung by official criticism of his aircraft, Lavochkin was hastily looking for ways to save his 'baby' by the autumn of 1941. Meanwhile, more than 400 new 1,700hp M-82 radial engines designed by Arkadiy Shvetsov had accumulated at Engine Factory No. 19 in Perm. Examples of this powerplant had by then been flight-tested in the MiG-3 and Yak-7 (both normally fitted with inline engines), although neither type had shown a great improvement in speed when paired with the M-82.

Now, with the NKAP seeking to solve the problems surrounding the supply of Klimov engines, it requested that the LaGG-3 be paired up with alternate powerplant in the form of the readily available M-82 (designated the ASh-82 by the VVS-KA from the spring of 1944), despite the latter being almost one-and-a-half times heavier than the fighter's M-105P! Lavochkin calculated that installation of the Shvetsov in the LaGG-3 was only possible after the fighter's slender airframe had been drastically reworked. Indeed, the diameter of the M-82 was 18in. greater than the maximum cross-section of the LaGG-3's fuselage. And as previously mentioned, it was 551lb heavier and significantly shorter than the M-105P, which in turn meant that the fighter's centre of gravity would be shifted dangerously forwards.

Despite these problems, an engineering team from Plant No. 21 led by Semyon Alexeyev set about modifying a production LaGG-3 fuselage to accept an M-82. The task proved to be an extremely complicated one, but after many weeks they had created a radial-engined fighter. Because the M-82's mid-section was much wider than the fuselage of the LaGG-3, a plywood skirting was bonded to both sides of the fuselage's load-carrying skin. The engine mounts were reworked to take the new engine and ShVAK 20mm synchronised cannons fitted above the M-82. Finally, engine cooling was achieved by the installation of two variable cooling flaps on the fuselage sides, the M-82's cooling-air baffles (surfaces which regulated the flow of cooling air for the engine's cylinders) being slightly modified so as to provide uniform thermal conditions for the upper and lower cylinders.

The new fighter, designated the LaGG-3 M-82, was rolled out of the Gorkiy plant in February 1942, and by early March it was ready for its first flight. The latter event was undertaken by Plant No. 21 test pilot G. A. Mishchenko, who told an anxious Lavochkin upon his return that 'The aircraft is good, pleasant to control and responsive, but the cylinder heads become hot. Measures should be taken to correct this'. Further test flights confirmed this problem, the M-82 overheating even when the outside air temperature was below zero. The oil cooler was subsequently replaced with a more efficient design, the supercharger air intake repositioned in the upper section

# La-7

29ft 2.5in.

8ft 6.25in.

32ft 1.75in.

of the cowling and the baffles were improved. On a more positive note, early testing had also shown the LaGG-3 M-82's speed to be 372mph in level flight at medium to low altitudes – some 37mph faster than a production-standard LaGG-3.

By mid-April 1942 the most serious problems afflicting the new aircraft had been solved, and it was handed over to the VVS NII KA for testing. Further evaluation was undertaken in May, when the LaGG-3 M-82 outperformed not only indigenous fighter types but also captured enemy aircraft too. At the conclusion of the test period VVS NII KA Chief Engineer Gen A. K. Repin noted 'The first experiment in using an M-82 engine in a LaGG fighter aircraft has produced satisfactory results – flight and technical personnel give the LaGG-5 a positive evaluation'. The VVS NII KA recommended that the fighter be put into series production at Plant No. 21, and this was officially approved by the State Committee for Defence on 19 May 1942.

Although the tests had proven the soundness of the design, they had also highlighted some problems. The fighter was even more difficult to fly than the notoriously poor-handling LaGG-3. This was particularly the case when changing direction in a banked turn, the pilot needing great physical strength to cope with the stick forces required to perform such a manoeuvre. It also took 25 seconds to complete a banked turn – too long for a single-engined fighter. This was primarily because the fighter was overweight. Engine oil splashing on the windscreen and 'supercooling', which saw the M-82 stall due to power loss, were also regular afflictions.

Nevertheless, production LaG-5s (as the aircraft was now designated – this was shortened to La-5 in September 1942) started to leave Factory No. 21 from July, with the first examples to reach the frontline being issued to 49th Red Banner IAP.

In the autumn of 1942 the VVS first documented the appearance at the front of new German fighters in the form of the Bf 109G-2 and Fw 190A-3. Both aircraft had a maximum speed of more than 380mph in level flight, while the La-5 could only accelerate up to 362mph at an altitude of 20,000ft. In an effort to achieve parity with the new breed of Luftwaffe fighters, Shvetsov introduced the M-82 *forsirovannyi* ('boosted') engine in December 1942. Improvements to its durability meant that pilots could now build up supercharger boost pressure without suffering the mechanical woes that often afflicted the engine – previously, using boost for more than five minutes was forbidden, as it tended to burn through the exhaust pipes. Improving the engine's performance by 160hp, the new powerplant made the Lavochkin fighter more effective up to 10,000ft. The 'boosted' engine was installed in the La-5F at Gorkiy from January 1943.

Initially, unmodified La-5 airframes were fitted with the new engines. However, Lavochkin had also been working on aerodynamic improvements to his fighter, giving the pilot a better view from the

Fresh-faced groundcrewmen are instructed on the inner workings of an M-82F *forsirovannyi* ('boosted') radial engine fitted to an La-5F.

cockpit. The La-5's poor handling characteristics in certain flight regimes were also addressed, and the aircraft underwent a strict weight reduction programme, which included decreasing the fighter's fuel capacity from five to three internal tanks. The end result was the definitive La-5F, which had lowered rear fuselage decking, sealed cowling joints, reshaped oil cooler ducts and myriad other detail changes. Armament consisted of two ShVAK 20mm cannons. These changes gave the aircraft a top speed of 364mph at 12,000ft, which made it faster than the Fw 190A-4 at this altitude.

Just as the new variant was entering production, Shvetsov commenced testing the M-82FN at his Perm factory, this engine featuring direct fuel injection into the cylinders. Although 66lb heavier than the M-82F, the new engine produced 1,850hp – 150hp more than its predecessor. Lavochkin also improved the La-5 to take advantage of the new powerplant, introducing fuselage pressurisation, a retractable tail wheel and larger tail surfaces to reduce stick forces when manoeuvring.

The La-5FN first saw combat with 32nd GIAP of 1st GIAK (Guards Fighter Aviation Corps) on the Bryansk Front in July–August 1943. Participating in the bitter aerial engagements over the Kursk Bulge, the unit completed 25 combat missions and claimed 33 aircraft destroyed (including 21 Fw 190As) for the loss of six La-5FNs – it is likely that these successes were seriously exaggerated. Nevertheless, the Luftwaffe quickly realised that the latest incarnation of the Lavochkin fighter was to be avoided at medium to low altitudes.

With La-5FN production finally getting into full swing by late 1943 following restricted availability of M-82FN engines, Lavochkin set about further refining his by now outstanding fighter. Dubbed the '1944 standard' aircraft, the new aircraft had metal rather than wooden wing spars, improved internal and external sealing of the powerplant to the airframe and three 20mm UB-20 cannons. The fighter's oil cooler was also relocated from the bottom of the engine cowling to the underside of the rear fuselage and the supercharger air intake moved from atop the cowling to the wing centre section leading edges. Flown for the first time on 1 February 1944, the '1944 standard' aircraft was 121lb lighter than the La-5FN. This meant that a top speed of 425mph could be attained at 20,200ft (making it 50mph faster than the Fw 190A-8 at this altitude), despite the aircraft using a standard 1,850hp M-82FN engine.

Although possessing promising performance, the new aircraft also suffered a series of problems during further testing that slowed its introduction into service.

ABOVE LEFT: A quartet of La-5FNs have their M-82FN engines run up on a snow-covered airfield during the early months of 1944. All four machines have the distinctive FN diamond marking on their tightly fitting engine cowlings.

ABOVE RIGHT: For much of the war all Lavochkin fighters were armed with a pair of 20mm ShVAK cannons synchronised to fire through the propeller – two ammunition cans contained a total of 400 rounds for the ShVAKs. In the final months of the conflict a number of new-build La-7s had their ShVAKs replaced by three Berezina UB-20 cannons.

An early-build La-7 from an unidentified unit rests between sorties in late 1944. The fighter's key recognition feature was its clean cowling, devoid of the La-5FN's extended supercharger intake trunk fairing and engine oil cooler intake.

The principal fault centred on the UB-20 cannon, as in certain flight profiles spent cartridges from the weapons hit the fighter's tail fin when ejected. It was decided that the aircraft, designated the La-7, would keep the La-5FN's weaponry.

Production of the aircraft commenced at Gorkiy in the spring of 1944, followed by Plant No. 381 in Moscow. Service testing by 63rd GIAP started in mid-September, with 30 aircraft being assigned to the regiment. The latter had flown the La-5 since late 1942, so both pilots and groundcrew quickly converted to the new fighter. These early machines suffered from poor engine reliability, and four La-7s were lost through powerplant failure. This was being caused by the ingestion of sand and dust into the cylinders through the La-7's relocated air intake. The armament was also causing problems, as the reworking of the cowling area made the guns less accessible for reloading. The hitting power of the weapons was also criticised, as a single burst of fire was proving insufficient to down an Fw 190 even from close range. However, the most serious problem was the spate of in-flight wing failures that resulted in six crashes and the death of four pilots in late October 1944. The La-7 was grounded until the fault (reduced density of the metal used to build the spars) was found.

These technical issues were eventually overcome, and by war's end more than 5,750 La-7s had been built. The last of these were fitted with three synchronised Berezina UB-20 cannons, production of this variant having finally commenced in January 1945.

# Fw 190

Arguably, the Focke-Wulf Fw 190 evolved into wartime Germany's most effective fighter, offering the Luftwaffe the benefit of manoeuvrability combined with stability as a formidable gun platform and the flexibility to perform as an air superiority fighter, a heavily armed and armoured interceptor and as an ordnance-carrying ground-attack aircraft. Yet the development of the Fw 190 was often protracted and tortuous. Following a specification by the *Technisches Amt* (Technical Office) of the *Reichsluftfahrtministerium* (RLM) in 1937 to Focke-Wulf Flugzeugbau GmbH for a fighter with a performance that would be superior to that of the still new and largely untested Bf 109, Dipl.-Ing. Kurt Tank, the firm's Technical Director, and his design team at Bremen dutifully turned to the drawing board. Tank described his approach to the development of the fighter as follows:

> The 'aircraft-soldier' should be simple and undemanding, capable of operating from rough, frontline airfields, easy for flight/technical staff to familiarise themselves with, able to 'hold its ground' and return to its home base after sustaining considerable battle

damage and carry powerful weaponry. Therefore, ideologically, the Fw 190 is not a 'racing stallion' but a simple, strong and sturdy 'cavalier's horse'.

Yet before the first project drawings of the 'cavalier's horse' were issued there were voices of discontent – not from Messerschmitt or other manufacturers, but from within the RLM itself. There were those who considered the Bf 109 to be of such advanced design that it would be impossible to develop and construct another fighter of comparable performance and quality. In any case, claimed the dissenters, any future war involving German arms would not last long enough to justify the time and expense of its development, or to find the aircraft sufficient employment. Furthermore, Focke-Wulf's response was to think in terms of a rugged aircraft built first and foremost for *interception*, and therefore able to absorb considerable punishment in action, not specifically for *offence* or *attack*. This philosophy won little support in the corridors of the RLM, however.

German air doctrine at this stage envisaged a short war – weeks or months at the most, with an enemy defeated by swift movement and overwhelming force – and debate coursed through the RLM as to the Focke-Wulf proposal. Many believed that there would be no requirement for an aircraft whose *raison d'être* was essentially that of *defence*, let alone one which incorporated apparently highly dubious, heavy and expensive radial engine technology in preference to a more aerodynamically favourable inline, liquid-cooled engine.

However, Tank, a decorated war veteran, and Focke-Wulf's resolute and exceptionally gifted designer, remained undaunted, and within some quarters of the *Technisches Amt* he found support. Because an air-cooled radial was capable of withstanding more combat stress (a single bullet hole could sever a coolant line and rapidly cause a liquid-cooled inline engine to seize up through overheating), and because Tank's design would not impinge upon production of the liquid-cooled DB 601 – the powerplant of the Bf 109 – the RLM eventually relented and permitted the Focke-Wulf design to proceed.

In the summer of 1938 the RLM issued a contract for construction of three prototypes of the 'Fw 190', a single-seat fighter to be powered by the 18-cylinder, 1,550hp BMW 139 radial engine. Maintaining the tradition of naming its machines after birds, Focke-Wulf came to know the Fw 190 as the '*Würger*' ('Shrike'). Drawings of the V1 dating from the autumn of 1938 show proposals to install an armament of two 7.9mm MG 17 and two 13mm MG 131 machine guns, all wing-mounted.

Focke-Wulf took its time and made strenuous efforts to ensure that structure and build were second to none, and that the design would demand the minimum of maintenance in operational conditions. Early on it was realised that the BMW 139 was suffering from teething problems, and

The very first of the line. This is the Fw 190 V1 undergoing final assembly in the Focke-Wulf Bremen plant in the spring of 1939. The unusual ducted spinner with its large circular central intake area is particularly visible. Noticeable around the aircraft are components of another of Focke-Wulf's contemporary products, the Fw 189 twin-engine, twin-boom reconnaissance aircraft. It is possible that the aircraft (just visible) behind the Fw 190 V1 could be the Fw 189 V4, which approximated to the layout of the Fw 189A production series.

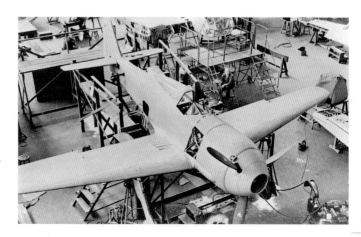

A BMW 801D-2 fitted in an Fw 190A. The whole powerplant arrangement was neat and closely cowled, being one of the finest examples of radial engine installation in a World War II fighter. This aircraft has 'tropical' filters fitted to its open-fronted supercharger air intakes (the large pipe-like structure beneath the open side cowling panel)

this would prove to be the main fault in an otherwise exemplary prototype by the time the unarmed Fw 190 V1 flew for the first time on 1 June 1939. Focke-Wulf's chief test pilot, Hans Sander, was nearly suffocated by exhaust fumes from an overheating engine that reached a temperature of more than 130° F during the flight.

BMW quickly offered a replacement in the form of the BMW 801, which was another radial engine of the same diameter, but longer and heavier by 350lb. This necessitated moving the cockpit further back and strengthening the airframe, which helped alleviate the problem. However, Luftwaffe engineers noted that the whole project would hinge on the performance of the 1,600hp BMW 801. Problems still occurred with the new powerplant too, and in the case of the armed V6, the engine temperature soared to the extent that the ammunition in the cowl machine guns became dangerously hot during test flying.

Focke-Wulf was fortunate in that no less a figure than Reichsmarschall Hermann Göring happened to be present when the BMW 801C-0-equipped fifth prototype flew with a reworked fuselage from Bremen in April 1940. It quickly became evident that the alterations to the design adversely affected wing loading, and thus manoeuvrability, but Göring apparently viewed the new aircraft with enthusiasm. Indeed, his endorsement provided the catalyst for the further production of a series of six Fw 190A-0s, and these were delivered to the test unit *Erprobungsstaffel* 190, under Oberleutnant Otto Behrens, at Rechlin in late February 1941.

Difficulties were initially encountered with these machines. Occasionally the propeller mechanism proved troublesome, but it was the BMW 801C that caused the most headaches. Between the arrival of the Fw 190A-0s and the early summer, Behrens, a trained motor mechanic, and his engineers and pilots (most of the latter seconded from II./JG 26) undertook intensive trouble-shooting in an effort to improve engine reliability – powerplants were routinely failing after just 20 flying hours, the BMWs erupting in flames. Finally, by August 1941, things were deemed safe enough to allow the first Fw 190A-1 production machines, each armed with four Rheinmetall-Borsig MG 17s (two in the cowling and two in the wing roots) and a pair of 20mm Oerlikon MG FF cannons in the outer wings, to be handed over to 6./JG 26 in Belgium.

Unfortunately, despite the best efforts of *Erprobungsstaffel* 190, problems persisted – nine Fw 190s crashed in August–September, and according to Behrens' reports, the finger of blame was pointed at BMW, whose engines continued to be plagued by overheating and compressor damage. There were also further delays in the delivery of the much anticipated 801D, these again being caused by mechanical failures.

Towards the end of 1941 deliveries of the Fw 190A-2 to Major Gerhard Schöpfel's *Stab./*JG 26 at Audembert and Major Johannes Seifert's I./JG 26 at St Omer commenced, this time in greater numbers than the A-1, since Focke-Wulf was supplemented in its output from Bremen by sub-contractors Ago in Oschersleben and Arado at Warnemünde.

The A-2 benefited from an improved 1,600hp BMW 801C-2 that was cooled by extra ventilation slots at the rear of the engine. The aircraft also featured an uprated weapons array that included two 20mm Mauser MG 151 cannons built into the wing roots, with interrupter gear incorporated to allow synchronised fire through the propeller arc. The aircraft was fitted with a Revi C/12D reflector gunsight, FuG 7 transmitter/receivers and FuG 25 IFF (identification friend/foe) equipment. The production lines delivered 425 Fw 190A-2s between August 1941 and July 1942.

Three months earlier, in April 1942, the first examples of the Fw 190A-3 had been delivered to JG 26, with Ago and Arado having been engaged in production since late the previous year. The A-3 was fitted with the new 1,700hp BMW 801D-2 engine, its uprated power achieved by increasing the compression ratio in the cylinders and refining the two-speed supercharger. The variant was also equipped with a pair of MG 17s and two MG 151s, and it also featured a modified tail fin to accommodate an aerial antenna, as well as a redesigned cowling. Production of the A-3 continued into 1943, by which time 509 had been built. The A-3 was graced with the ability to adapt easily to the role of a fighter-bomber using a series of *Umbau* (modifications) – as the A-3/U1 (by means of installation of an ETC 500 bomb rack), U3 (ETC 250 fuselage rack and SC 50 underwing racks) and U7 sub-variants.

The Fw 190A-4 was developed into a fully 'convertible fighter/fighter-bomber', with low-level capability provided by an Methanol-Water (MW) 50 power boost system when flying below 16,500ft. Capitalising on the A-3's adaptability, the Fw 190A-4, although carrying the same fixed armament as its predecessor, introduced an even more wide-ranging and sophisticated family of sub-variants. The A-4/U1, armed with only two MG 151s, was fitted with a pair of ETC 501 bomb racks for carrying two SC 250 bombs, while the A-4/U3 emerged in October 1942 as a true 'assault' aircraft. It boasted a 6mm armoured ring ahead of the cowling and 5mm steel armour plates beneath the cowling and cockpit that were designed to protect the pilot, fuel tanks and engine on ground-attack missions. The A-4/U8 was a long-range fighter-bomber fitted with a 66-gallon drop tank and four SC 50 bombs on wing racks, together with full armament. Benefiting from an MW 50 power boost system, the A-4 also carried a FuG 16Z VHF transceiver.

From April 1943 the Fw 190A-4 was superseded by the A-5. With the exception of a lengthened fuselage (by 6in.) and strengthened housing for the BMW 801D-2 engine, the A-5, of which 723 were built up to the summer of 1943, was essentially unaltered, but

Seemingly oblivious to the roar of the BMW 801D-2 ticking over just feet away from them, two suitably insulated 'black men' turn their thoughts to Bavaria in July. The pilot, meanwhile, has gone 'head down' in the cockpit in order to check that the engine oil temperature is rising correctly in his Fw 190A-4 prior to undertaking I./JG 54's first sortie of the day from Krasnogvardeisk in early 1943. Once his dials indicate that the radial powerplant has 'warmed to the occasion', he will wave away both the trolley acc, parked behind the fighter, and the wheel chocks and then taxi out to the ice runway for take-off.

offered an even more inventive selection of sub-variants, reflecting the versatility of the fighter. Provision was made for cannons, drop tanks, fuselage/wing-mounted bombs and 21cm underwing air-to-air mortars for operations against US heavy bombers.

The fighter-bomber and attack aircraft variants that would feature so prominently on the Eastern Front were based on the Fw 190A-5. Indeed, in July 1943 an Fw 190A-5/U3 attack aircraft was captured by the Soviets and handed over to the VVS NII KA for evaluation. Its specialists established that apart from the usual armour protection weighing 242lb, A-5/U3 aircraft also carried 16 additional armour plates totalling 441lb.

Attack versions of the Fw 190A had started to arrive on the Eastern Front with Luftwaffe *Schlachtgruppen* from March 1943, and these were routinely engaged by La-5/7 pilots through to war's end. Based on the Fw 190A-5/U8, the G-1 was equipped with racks under the fuselage to carry bombs up to a weight of 4,000lb. Strengthened landing gear was introduced to allow the Fw 190G to cope with the extra weight. The G-2 and G-3 differed only in the type of wing racks they used for their external stores, and they started to reach frontline units in the late summer of 1943. The final variant was the G-8, produced from the autumn of 1943 through to the spring of 1944. Powered by an uprated 1,800hp BMW 801D-2 engine and incorporating upgrades introduced in the Fw 190A-8, this version, fitted with a nitrous oxide injection system, was designated the Fw 190G-8/R4.

Entering service after the G-1, the Fw 190F-1 was based on the A-4. Its outboard wing cannons were removed and 793lb of armour plating fitted to protect the engine and cockpit from groundfire. This variant was further modified to carry a centreline ETC 501 bomb rack. The follow-on F-2 was related to the Fw 190A-5 but it introduced a bubble canopy, while the F-3, which corresponded to the Fw 190A-6, could carry a 66-gallon drop tank or 550lb bomb on its centreline. F-3/R1 and R2 sub-variants had additional wing racks or MK 103 30mm cannon options. The F-8 was based on the Fw 190A-8, with two engine-mounted MG 131 machine guns and ETC 50 bomb racks. The F-8/U2 and U3 had a TSA bombsight for anti-shipping strikes with, respectively, the BT 700 or BT 1400 bombs. The final Fw 190F variant was the F-9, which was similar to the F-8 but powered by the BMW 801 TS/TH.

The factor of weight provided the genesis for the first variant in a series that saw Focke-Wulf redesign certain elements in the Fw 190, such as internal wing structure,

Bombs gone from their ventral racks, a pair of Fw 190Fs – possibly from II./SG 77 – return to base somewhere in the southern Russian steppe in the spring of 1944.

# Fw 190A-6

28ft 10.5in.

12ft 11.5in.

34ft 5.5in.

The Fw 190A-6 introduced a considerable up-gunning of the A-series, with the addition of an MG 151 20mm cannon in each outer weapons station in the mid-wing location just outboard of the main undercarriage attachment. This aircraft illustrates the A-6 layout, although it is possibly an A-5/U10 development aircraft that was used as a layout for the A-6 production version. The Focke-Wulf photograph was released for publication on 8 December 1944, but was taken well before that time.

in order to allow for greater capability and adaptation in ordnance load. Units in the field had found that the MG FF outer wing cannons did not provide sufficient firepower, and simply added weight on the A-5. Thus emerged the Fw 190A-6.

Originally conceived as a fighter for the Eastern Front, the A-6 was designed to accept an array of *Rustsätze* (field conversion kits) that could be added quickly to, or removed from, an airframe for mission flexibility. The A-6 went into production in May 1943, and up to February 1944 1,192 machines had been built by Arado at Warnemünde, Ago at Oschersleben and Fieseler at Kassel. The aircraft was fitted with a 1,700hp BMW 801D-2. The standard fuel load – and thus range – was enhanced by the installation of a centreline ETC 501 bomb rack, to which could be hung a 66-gallon drop tank. Standard armament consisted of two fuselage-mounted 7.92mm MG 17 machine guns (replaced with MG 131s in the A-7) and four electrically fired 20mm Mauser MG 151/20 cannons. The tracer ammunition of the former weapon allowed Luftwaffe pilots to sharpen their aim when using the latter.

The heavier armed, and armoured, versions of the Fw 190A-6, A-7 and A-8 were used almost exclusively by Defence of the Reich units in the west (although IV./JG 3 used its anti-bomber Fw 190A-8/R8s in strafing attacks on Soviet troops as the latter advanced on Berlin), and are therefore not detailed in this volume.

The Fw 190A-8 was by far the most numerous and most potent of all the BMW-engined Focke-Wulf fighter variants. Indeed, more than 2,500 examples were produced between Focke-Wulf at Cottbus and Aslau, Ago at Oschersleben, Fieseler at Kassel, Weserflug at Tempelhof and Norddeutsche Dornier at Wismar.

Also powered by a BMW 801D-2, it could attain a maximum speed of 404mph at 18,000ft, reaching 410mph with GM 1 nitrous oxygen boost. Fuel was held in two self-sealing tanks (of 51 and 64 gallons respectively) beneath the cockpit, but another 25 gallons could be carried in the area normally assigned to the GM 1 fuel tank or the MW 50 methanol-water boost. Range was 646 miles at 23,000ft, extending to 920 miles when carrying a 66-gallon drop tank.

The last all-new variant of the Focke-Wulf fighter to engage La-5/7s in the final months of the war was the Fw 190D-9. Developed in 1942 as a replacement for the aborted Fw 190B/C high altitude fighter, the *Langnasen-Dora* ('Longnose-Dora') made use of the inverted inline Junkers Jumo 213 engine, combined with an MW 50 booster, to achieve an impressive rate of climb and top speed – crucial ingredients for a Defence of the Reich fighter. Service entry came in August 1944, with the first fighters to reach the Jagdwaffe being used as Me 262 airfield defenders. Although most D-9s served in the west, a small number from JGs 3, 4, 6 and 51 saw sporadic action in the ill-fated defence of Berlin in the last months of the war, and claims were made by some of the higher scoring aces against the best Soviet fighters of the day.

# TECHNICAL SPECIFICATIONS

## La-5/7

### LaGG-3 M-82

This experimental aircraft was created when a standard production LaGG-3 had its water-cooled Klimov M-105P engine replaced with a Shvetsov M-82A radial by an engineering team from Plant No. 21 in Gorkiy in February 1942. The air-cooled powerplant weighed 1,895lb and produced 1,700hp at low level, 1,540hp at an altitude of 6,725ft and 1,330hp at 17,700ft. By contrast, the output of the M-105P did not exceed 1,100hp at any altitude. The diameter of the M-82 was 18in. greater than the cross-section of the M-105P, and this meant that the LaGG-3's forward fuselage had to be reworked in order to accommodate the engine. The aircraft was to have been armed with four ShVAK 20mm cannons, but problems with engine cooling meant that two of them had to be removed so that two variable cooling flaps could be added to the fuselage sides. First flown in March 1942, the aircraft was subsequently destroyed in a crash on 12 July 1942 following engine failure.

The LaGG-3 M-82 experimental aircraft is seen with its cowlings open to reveal the snug-fitting Shvetsov M-82 radial engine. This one-off machine was created by an engineering team from Plant No. 21 in Gorkiy in February 1942, the standard production LaGG-3 having its water-cooled Klimov M-105P engine replaced with the Shvetsov radial.

## LaG-5

This variant of the aircraft was produced from the end of July to 8 September 1942 at Gorkiy's Factory No. 21. The first 200 aircraft had a forward

Two La-5s and an La-5F (closest to the camera, with a small letter 'F' in a circle on its engine cowling) sit at readiness on the Russian steppe during the spring of 1943. These aircraft could be in the air within minutes of being told to scramble.

fuselage section made of double-thickness bakelite ply (layers of birch strip bonded with bakelite film) skinning, which could be shaped to provide smooth contours from the circular engine cowling forward of the cockpit through to the oval framing of the rear fuselage and tail section. New technology in the manufacturing process introduced with the LaG-5 meant that the fighter's weight was reduced by 188lb in comparison with the LaGG-3 M-82. In contrast to the prototype, the wings of production aircraft featured leading edge slats on the outer sections. The fuel system consisted of five tanks, four of them in the wings. Some aircraft were manufactured with a single ShVAK cannon and a Berezin UBS 12.7mm machine gun.

## La-5

The LaG-5 became the La-5 following order number 683, dated 8 September 1942, from NKAP. Virtually identical to its predecessor, the fighter was built at Plant No. 21 from September 1942 through to the end of that year, by which time 1,107 La-5s had been constructed – a further 22 were completed by Factory No. 31 in Tbilisi. The fighter had a maximum speed of 355mph at an altitude of 6,500ft and 362mph at 18,500ft. Complaints from former LaGG-3 pilots that the LaG-5's heavier weight and insufficient control surface size and balance made it more demanding to fly led to an increase in the size of the elevator and the tail fin in production La-5s, although the horizontal tailplane area remained the same. Flat armoured glass 57mm thick was added to the windscreen, while external store shackles were also introduced.

## La-5F

NKAP order number 778, dated 16 September 1942, instructed aircraft engine Factory No. 19 in Molotov to commence production of the M-82F *forsirovannyi* ('boosted') engine. Its improved supercharger boost only worked up to an altitude of 10,000ft, its output at an altitude of 2,600ft having been increased to 1,760hp. Aircraft fitted with this engine had their cowling flaps inscribed with a small letter 'F' in a circle (this was later changed to a diamond shape). The supercharger intake trunk fairing atop the engine cowling was increased in size so as to channel more air to the M-82F. Additionally, every second La-5F was fitted with an RSI-4 radio set.

More significantly, in an effort to improve visibility, the fighter's rear fuselage decking behind the cockpit was lowered and the canopy lengthened, with a transparent rear section fitted with armoured glass. These aircraft were given the identifier 'Type 39'

This late production La-5F has the cutdown rear fuselage decking that drastically improved the pilot's rearward visibility. Soviet fighter pilots habitually flew with their canopies open, and this was particularly the case in regiments equipped with the La-5, as the air temperature in a closed cockpit quickly became excessive due to poor ventilation.

at Factory No. 21, with the modification first being seen on the ninth batch of La-5Fs built in November 1942. Factory No. 21 was joined in production of the La-5F by Factory No. 99 in Ulan-Ude and Factory No. 381 in Nizhniy Tagil from January 1943.

## La-5FN

Bench testing of the M-82FN engine with fuel injection at Shvetsov's Perm factory was completed by late June 1942. The M-82 had shown a propensity for overheating due to the La-5's close-fitting cowlings, so the FN version was re-engineered with enlarged cylinder ribbing to improve cooling in-flight. Internally, its pistons and rods were also reinforced and every cylinder was fitted with an individual exhaust pipe. Finally, the

## La-5FN CANNONS

All versions of the La-5, and most La-7s, were armed with two synchronised ShVAK 20mm cannons, each weapon having its own ammunition tank containing 200 rounds per gun. The Lavochkin fighter was originally to have been armed with four synchronised ShVAKs, but problems with engine cooling meant that two of the weapons had to be removed so that two variable cooling flaps could be added to the fuselage sides. Some early-build LaG-5s were also manufactured with a single ShVAK cannon and one large-calibre Berezin UBS 12.7mm machine gun. Whilst Soviet pilots rarely complained about the reliability of their weaponry, the two synchronised ShVAK cannons occasionally proved insufficient to knock down the well-armoured Fw 190.

23

engine featured direct fuel injection into the cylinder heads in place of the carburettors fitted to the M-82 and M-82F. The engine's output increased to 1,850hp at low level, 1,670hp at 5,000ft and 1,460hp at 15,000ft.

The prototype La-5FN was first tested in December 1942, this aircraft being a highback 'Type 37' La-5. In March 1943 a second prototype La-5FN was built utilising the latest 'Type 39' airframe, and this was handed over for state testing at the end of that month. Featuring metal wing spars and a flight weight of just 7,000lb, the second prototype exhibited outstanding performance characteristics – a maximum speed of 372mph at low level using boost, 391mph at 10,500ft and 405mph at 20,500ft. Lavochkin made various improvements to the airframe to take advantage of the new powerplant, introducing fuselage pressurisation, a retractable tail wheel and larger tail surfaces to improve handling and reduce stick forces when manoeuvring. The radio mast was angled against the airflow and the air intake for the gear-driven supercharger was enlarged atop the engine cowling. The letters 'FN' within a diamond shape were inscribed on the sides of the engine nacelles.

In spite of its improved performance, the La-5FN was not put into immediate mass production because of a shortage of M-82FNs. Indeed, the Gorkiy plant had to wait until the autumn of 1943 before it had sufficient engines available to switch to La-5FN production. Other plants started building La-5FNs in early 1944.

## La-7

Initially dubbed the '1944 standard' La-5FN, this aircraft featured a number of significant differences from its immediate predecessor. The fighter had metal wing spars in place of wooden examples, improved internal and external sealing of the powerplant to the airframe and three 20mm UB-20 cannons. Its oil cooler was also relocated (from the bottom of the engine cowling to the underside of the rear fuselage) and the supercharger air intake moved from atop the cowling to the wing centre section leading edges. The aircraft's take-off weight had also been reduced by 121lb, and its aerodynamics improved. As a result, the prototype displayed outstanding performance characteristics, with a maximum speed of 373mph being achieved at low level, 419mph at 10,500ft and 425mph at 20,000ft.

Soon designated the La-7, production examples (classified as 'Type 45s' by Lavochkin) started to emerge from Gorkiy's Plant No. 21 in the spring of 1944, with Plant No. 381 in Moscow and Plant No. 99 in Ulan-Ude coming on line in April and September 1944, respectively. Aircraft were initially built with two ShVAK cannons rather than the planned trio of more modern UB-20s due to problems with the latter weapon. The La-7 remained in production until late 1945.

Officially captioned as 'an La-7 of an unidentified Guards regiment on the Baltic Front, 1944', this aircraft may have been the personal mount of Vasiliy Zaitsev (36 individual and 19 shared kills), deputy commander of 11th GIAD. Most of his fighters featured a white nose marking identical to the one seen here.

# Fw 190
## Fw 190 V1 and V2

The Fw 190 prototype was rolled out in May 1939 and flew for the first time from Bremen airfield on 1 June. The aircraft was powered by a fan-cooled 1,550hp BMW 139 radial fitted with a special ducted spinner to reduce drag, but the engine overheated rapidly nevertheless, and eventually the ducted spinner was removed and replaced by a new tightly-fitting NACA cowling. The Fw 190 V2 second prototype was also fitted with a large ducted spinner and powered by a BMW 139 engine. The latter was subsequently replaced by the longer and heavier BMW 801, which necessitated structural changes to the aircraft and the relocation of the cockpit. These prototypes were armed with two 13mm MG 131 machine guns in the wings and two 7.92mm MG 17 weapons in the upper forward fuselage. The third and fourth prototypes were abandoned.

Several Fw 190A-0 pre-production aircraft are seen here at Bremen. All the A-0s were manufactured at Focke-Wulf's Bremen plant. The nearest aircraft, Wk-Nr. 0010, was fitted with a BMW 801C-1 engine, unlike the C-0 model installed in most, if not all, preceding A-0 airframes. Its engine cowling is clearly marked to signify the slightly different powerplant.

## Fw 190 V5/V5G

Once powered by the newly developed 1,660hp BMW 801C-0 engine, the V2 was modified to take a wing of increased span. To compensate for the greater engine weight, the cockpit was moved further aft. With the introduction of the V5g ('g' standing for gross or large), the V5 short-span version (which had a wing area of 161.46 sq ft) was redesignated the Fw 190 V5k ('k' standing for klein or small). The V5k had a wing area of 196.98 sq ft.

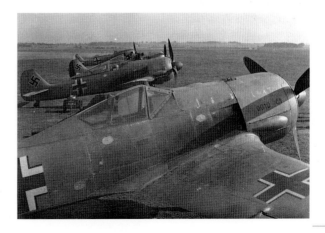

## Fw 190A-0

The pre-production batch, nine of these aircraft were fitted with the small wing, while the remainder had the larger-span version. 100 production Fw 190As were ordered, the first five of which bore the alternative designations V7 to V11.

## Fw 190A-1

This initial production model was essentially similar to the V5g, being powered by a 1,660hp BMW 801C-1 radial, having the long-span wing, 7.92mm MG 17 machine guns and FuG 7a radio equipment. In August 1941 the first Fw 190A-1s were delivered to *Stab./*JG 26.

## Fw 190A-2

The Fw 190 V14 first prototype had two 7.9mm MG 17 machine guns above the engine cowling and two 20mm MG FF cannons in the wing roots. The production Fw 190A-2, which was powered by the BMW 801C-2 engine, often carried an additional pair of MG 17 machine guns in the outboard wing panels.

## Fw 190A-3

The neat installation of the two Rheinmetall-Borsig MG 17 7.9mm machine guns in the upper forward fuselage weapons station of all production A-model Fw 190s up to and including the A-6.

This was the first major production variant to be powered by the 1,700hp BMW 801D-2. It had the MG FF cannons moved to the outer wing panels, and their original location used instead for two of the much faster-firing 20mm MG 151/20 weapons. The canopy could be jettisoned with the aid of explosive bolts and the pilot was protected by 12.7mm and 19mm armour plate. The first examples were introduced into service in autumn 1941.

## Fw 190A-4

Delivered during the late summer of 1942 with FuG 16Z radio and a fin-mounted radio mast atop the fin. The BMW 801D-2 had provision for MW 50 water-methanol fuel injection to boost output to 2,100hp for short periods, and thus raise the maximum speed to 416mph at 21,000ft.

## Fw 190A-4/R6

MW 50 deleted. Capable of carrying a pair of underwing Werfergranate

# Fw 190A-5 WING GUNS

The Fw 190A-5 packed a powerful punch when compared to its relatively lightly armed Soviet opponents. Oerlikon MG FF 20mm cannons (and their single 140-round ammunition boxes) were fitted in the outer weapons stations in the mid-wing area. The MG FFs proved to be less than reliable in service, and they were often removed in an effort to save weight. The MG FFs were replaced by Mauser MG 151 20mm cannons from the Fw 190A-6 onwards, these weapons having initially been fitted in the wing-root bays of the A-5 only. The two ammunition boxes for the wing-root cannons were housed within the fuselage behind the main spar, each magazine holding 250 rounds.

# Fw 190A-5 COWLING GUNS

A pair of Rheinmetall-Borsig MG 17 7.9mm machine guns were installed in the upper forward fuselage weapons station in all production A-model Fw 190s up to and including the A-6. These guns were often disparagingly known as 'door knockers' due to their inability to penetrate the armour fitted to Soviet aircraft, in particular the Il-2. The MG 17s were fed ammunition from two fuselage-mounted boxes that each contained up to 475 rounds per gun.

WGr. 21 210mm rocket launchers for the unguided WGr. 21 Dodel missile. Fixed armament was reduced to two MG 151/20s.

## Fw 190A-4/U5

Able to carry a 66-gallon drop tank beneath each wing and a 1,102lb bomb under the fuselage.

## Fw 190A-5

Introduced in early 1943, this version was similar to the A-4 but had a revised engine mounting that enabled the BMW 801D-2 to be fitted 6in. further forward in an attempt to cure a tendency for the engine to overheat. Many sub-variants were produced, including the U3 equipped with underwing and centreline bomb racks, the camera-toting U4 and fighter-bomber optimised U6, U8 and U11.

## Fw 190A-6

Developed from the experimental Fw 190A-5/U10 in June 1943. A redesigned, lighter wing could take four MG 151/20s whilst retaining the two MG 17s mounted above the engine. FuG 16ZE and FuG 25 radio equipment was also carried.

## Fw 190A-6/R1

Developed following successful trials with the Fw 190A-5/U12, this aircraft had six MG 151/20 cannons.

## Fw 190A-6/R3

Armed with two 30mm MK 103 cannons in underwing gondolas.

## Fw 190A-6/R6

The final A-6 variant, this aircraft could carry a 210mm Werfergranate WGr. 21 rocket tube beneath each wing.

## Fw 190A-7

Introduced in December 1943, and basically similar to the Fw 190A-6, the first prototype was the Fw 190A-5/U9, which had two MG 151/20 cannons in the wings

On 7 March 1943 I./JG 54's Fw 190A-4s were credited with no fewer than 59 Soviet aircraft destroyed, including three 'LaGG-5s'. Among that day's claimants (with a LaGG-3 and a 'LaGG-5', the latter being the very first of his 49 La-5 kills) was the pilot of this aircraft, Leutnant Walter Nowotny. Despite suffering terrible losses, the VVS-KA had become more adept at staging surprise hit and run raids on Luftwaffe airfields by early 1943, and take-offs and landings became times of great peril for Fw 190 pilots. Amongst the first things taught to new arrivals in the east was how to take-off from any position on the field, either from a standing start or taxiing, and how to land quickly and safely from a low-level formation. Here, Leutnant Nowotny does just that, skimming in low over a huge snow bank at Krasnogvardeisk.

and two 13mm MG 131 machine guns above the engine cowling. The second prototype (Fw 190 V35) was similar, but had four MG 151/20s in the wings and a strengthened undercarriage. It was later re-engined with a 2,000hp BMW 801F. The *Rüstsatz* (conversion pack) produced for the A-7 was similar to that for the A-6, with much emphasis being placed on the A-7/R6 with WGr. 21 rocket tubes.

## Fw 190A-8/R7

Fitted with an armoured cockpit for use by anti-bomber *Sturmgruppen*.

## Fw 190A-8/R11

All-weather fighter with heated canopy and PKS 12 radio navigation equipment.

## Fw 190F-1

A dedicated ground attack version of the A-4, this aircraft had its outboard wing cannons removed and 793lb of armour plating fitted to protect the engine and cockpit from groundfire. The F-1 could also carry a centreline ETC 501 bomb rack.

## Fw 190F-2/3

The F-2 was related to the A-5, but it introduced a bubble canopy, while the F-3, which corresponded to the A-6, could carry a 66-gallon drop tank or 550lb bomb on its centreline. F-3/R1 and R2 had wing racks or MK 103 30mm cannon options.

## Fw 190F-8/9

The F-8 was based on the A-8, with two engine-mounted MG 131s and ETC 50 bomb racks. The F-8/U2 and U3 had a TSA bombsight for anti-shipping strikes with, respectively, BT 700 or BT 1400 bombs. The final Fw 190F variant was the F-9, which was similar to the F-8 but powered by the BMW 801 TS/TH engine.

In January 1945 the bulged-canopy Fw 190F-9s of II./SG 2, based in Hungary, wore distinctive and individual winter camouflage schemes. Aircraft from this unit were routinely intercepted by La-5FNs and La-7s during this period.

## Fw 190G-1

Based on the Fw 190A-5/U8, the G-1 was equipped with bomb racks under the fuselage to carry bombs up to a weight of 3,970lb. Strengthened landing gear was introduced to allow the Fw 190G to cope with the extra weight.

## Fw 190G-2/3

The G-2 and G-3 differed only in the type of wing racks used for their external stores, the former employing Messerschmitt-built racks and the latter Focke-Wulf equipment.

## Fw 190G-8

The final variant was the G-8, powered by an uprated 1,800hp BMW 801D-2 and incorporating upgrades introduced in the Fw 190A-8. This version, fitted with a nitrous oxide injection system, was designated the Fw 190G-8/R4.

## Fw 190D-9

The last all-new variant of the Focke-Wulf fighter to engage La-5/7s in the final months of the war was the Fw 190D-9. Developed in 1942 as a replacement for the aborted Fw 190B/C high altitude fighters, the *Langnasen-Dora* ('Longnose-Dora') made use of the exceptional 2,000hp inverted inline Junkers Jumo 213 engine, combined with an MW 50 water-methanol booster, to achieve an impressive rate of climb and top speed. Only 700 had been built by war's end, and very few were encountered on the Eastern Front in the final months of the conflict.

Smart, newly built Fw 190D-9 Wk-Nr. 210051 with a straight-topped cockpit cover from the first production batch of D-9 airframes. The completely changed nose contours of the Junkers Jumo 213-powered 'Dora-9' compared to the BMW 801-engined Fw 190 models, plus the lengthened rear fuselage, are evident in this view.

## La-5FN AND Fw 190A-4 COMPARISON SPECIFICATIONS

|  | La-5FN | Fw 190A-4 |
|---|---|---|
| Powerplant | 1,850hp ASh-82FN | 1,700hp BMW 801D-2 |
| **Dimensions** | | |
| Span | 32ft 1.78in. | 34ft 5.5in. |
| Length | 28ft 2.75in. | 28ft 10.5in. |
| Height | 8ft 4in. | 12ft 11.5in. |
| Wing area | 188.37 sq ft | 196.98 sq ft |
| **Weights** | | |
| Empty | 6,173lb | 6,393lb |
| Loaded | 7,407lb | 8,770lb |
| **Performance** | | |
| Max speed | 403mph at 20,670ft | 418mph at 21,000ft (with override boost) |
| Range | 360 miles | 497 miles |
| Rate of climb to 16,500ft | 4.7 min | 5.83 min |
| Service ceiling | 31,170ft | 34,775ft |
| **Armament** | 2 x 20mm ShVAK | 2 x 7.9mm MG 17<br>2 x 20mm MG 151/20<br>2 x 20mm FF |

## La-7 AND Fw 190D-9 COMPARISON SPECIFICATIONS

|  | La-7 | Fw 190D-9 |
|---|---|---|
| Powerplant | 1,850hp ASh-82FN | 2,000hp Junkers Jumo 213 |
| **Dimensions** | | |
| Span | 32ft 1.75in. | 34ft 5in. |
| Length | 29ft 2.5in. | 33ft 5in. |
| Height | 8ft 6.25in. | 11ft 0.25in. |
| Wing area | 189.35 sq ft | 197 sq ft |
| **Weights** | | |
| Empty | 5,842lb | 7,694lb |
| Loaded | 7,496lb | 10,670lb |
| **Performance** | | |
| Max speed | 423mph at 20,000ft | 426mph at 21,650ft |
| Range | 413 miles | 520 miles |
| Rate of climb to 16,500ft | 5.1 min | 4.9 min |
| Service ceiling | 37,000ft | 39,370ft |
| **Armament** | 2 or 3 x 20mm ShVAK or UB-20 | 2 x 13mm MG 131<br>2 x 20mm MG 151/20 |

# THE STRATEGIC SITUATION

Having helped with the defence of Stalingrad in late 1942, 240th IAP was one of the first regiments to trade its LaGG-3s for La-5s in 1943. It resumed operations on the Voronezh Front in March of that year, and in July participated in the Battle of Kursk.

By early September 1942 the first examples of the LaG-5 (the new aircraft had not yet been redesignated the La-5) had been combat tested by six fighter regiments of the Soviet VVS. Five of these units had been involved in the successful defence of Stalingrad as part of 287th IAD, while the sixth regiment, 49th IAP on the Western Front, had given the LaG-5 its combat debut the previous month. Their opponents for aerial supremacy at this time were the Bf 109F/G – these were the only German fighters then operating in the central and southern sectors of the Eastern Front.

During the second half of 1942, the VVS-KA had started to form all-new Fighter Air Corps within the Central Command Reserve, their regiments being equipped with the very latest fighters, bombers and attack aircraft available to the Soviets. 1st IAK, led by Gen E. M. Beletskiy, was ready for combat in the autumn, its 235th IAD being solely equipped with La-5s – its sister division, 274th IAD, flew Yak-7Bs, however. It was duly sent to the Kalinin Front, where the corps came under the control of 3rd *Vozdushnaya Armiya* (Air Army). No fewer than 78 La-5s (of which 68 were serviceable) were now committed to combat on the Kalinin Front – the largest concentration of Lavochkin fighters in VVS-KA at that time. A further 180 La-5s were in the process of being readied for frontline units, these machines being used to convert pilots onto the new fighter.

Early September had also seen the arrival of the first Fw 190A-3s in-theatre, and by coincidence these aircraft – assigned to I./JG 51 – had been sent to Lyuban, also on the Kalinin Front. Led by Hauptmann Heinrich Krafft, the *Gruppe* performed sweeps southeast of Leningrad. III./JG 51 (with II./JG 51's 6. *Staffel* attached, as its parent *Gruppe* had been rushed to North Africa following the Allied *Torch* landings) converted to the Fw 190 in December and returned to the Kalinin Front.

By then 235th IAD had been transferred out of 1st IAK, its place being taken by 210th IAD. Only one of its regiments (169th IAP, led by Maj I. P. Ivanov) was equipped with La-5s, 32 examples having been delivered to the unit directly from the factory in Gorkiy. According to figures published by division headquarters, 210th IAD had made 32 combat sorties and destroyed 53 aircraft – including six Fw 190As – by the end of December. Its own losses were 13 La-5s and two Yak-1s.

During this same period the Luftwaffe lost 12 Fw 190s from I./JG 51 to various causes. Most were downed by ground fire, with *Gruppenkommandeur* Hauptmann Krafft (a highly decorated ace with 78 victories to his name) falling victim to Soviet flak on 14 December. Despite the Focke-Wulf pilots' well founded belief in the survivability of their new aircraft and its rugged BMW radial – especially when compared with the liquid-cooled Daimler Benz engine in the Bf 109 – by the end of 1942 the squadron had lost 12 Fw 190As in combat and a further 26 in operational accidents. La-5 losses were around double this number in December 1942, although there were of course far more of them serving in frontline units at this point.

More Fw 190As were sent east in early 1943 as I. and III./JG 51 tried to provide support for the defenders of Velikiye Luki – the scene of one of three Soviet breakthroughs in German lines in November 1942. The *Gruppen* were also doing their best to shore up the Central Sector of the frontline as it came under repeated attack from seven Soviet armies supported by VVS-KA regiments. They got some support from late January 1943 when individual *Staffeln* from I. and II./JG 54 completed their conversion from the Bf 109F to the Fw 190A-4 and returned to snow-covered runways at Siverskaya and Krasnogvardeisk on the Leningrad front. Led by Hauptmann Hans Philipp, I. *Gruppe* in particular soon made its mark with the Fw 190 thanks to Feldwebel Otto Kittel and Leutnant Walter Nowotny. The two men would claim 525 victories between them, more than 70 of which were La-5/7s.

In mid-February 43 Fw 190A-5s landed at Ryelbitzi airfield, west of Lake Ilmen on the Kalinin Front. These machines were assigned to I./JG 26, the *Gruppe* being led by Major Johannes Seifert. Making its debut on the Eastern Front, I./JG 26 had been swapped with III./JG 54, which had been sent to Lille-Vendeville, in northern France, to operate on the Channel Front. In March IV./JG 51 replaced the last of its Bf 109Fs with Fw 190s, thus completing the re-equipment of fighter *Gruppen* on the Eastern Front. Those units still flying Bf 109Gs would continue to do so through to war's end. There were also a small number of Fw 190As serving with I. and IV./JG 5 in Norway, but these saw very little combat against the VVS-KA.

By the early spring Major Hubertus Hitschhold's I./SchlG 1 had also arrived at Kharkov, in the Southern Sector, with the first Fw 190F fighter-bombers to be seen in the east. Many more *Schlachtstaffeln* would receive Focke-Wulfs during the course

Hauptmann Heinrich Krafft was *Gruppenkommandeur* of I./JG 51 when it became the first unit to swap its Bf 109Fs for Fw 190As. A highly decorated ace with 78 victories to his name, he led the *Gruppe* back into action from Lyuban, on the Kalinin Front, in September 1942. 'Gaudi' Krafft did not last long, however, as he fell victim to Soviet flak on 14 December.

With its multiplicity of electrical systems, the Fw 190 embodied the very latest in German technology, but some things on the Eastern Front were best done the old way. And in Russia the panje pony, whether pulling a cart in summer or a sledge in winter, was an integral and indispensable part of life for Luftwaffe units such as I./JG 54 at Krasnogvardeisk in early 1943.

of the year, and by early 1944 *Schlacht* Fw 190Fs outnumbered Fw 190As in-theatre.

Meanwhile, the number of fighter regiments equipped with La-5s had also grown rapidly by April 1943. According to a VVS Central Headquarters report, the People's Commissariat for the Aviation Industry handed over 1,129 Lavochkin fighters in 1942. These numbers continued to increase in 1943, with 645 La-5Fs reaching frontline units in May alone. At the end of that month 13 air regiments were transferred into the VGK (Supreme High Command) fighter Reserve Air Corps and Air Armies, having completed their conversion onto the La-5. Each regiment had a complement of 32 fighters. In June the industry handed over a further 373 La-5Fs and, significantly, 36 uprated La-5FNs. The conversion of a further five air regiments onto the Lavochkin fighter was also underway at this time, thus allowing the VVS-KA to continue its strengthening on new air forces for the summer campaigns that were to come.

On the major fighting fronts of the Northern, Central and, to a much lesser extent, Southern Sectors, the full weight of the Fw 190 fighter presence in the USSR continued to be felt – if 'full weight' is the proper term to describe a force whose numbers never once topped the 200 mark along a front 1,200 miles in length! In fact, the weeks prior to the Kursk offensive were to see Fw 190 serviceability totals in Russia reach their all-time peak – 189 in May and 196 in June 1943.

On 5 July the long-awaited Operation *Zitadelle*, Hitler's last huge gamble to break the deadlock and turn the tide in the east once and for all, finally commenced. All but one of the five Fw 190 *Jagdgruppen* in the east were directly involved in *Zitadelle*. Leaving just Hauptmann Heinrich Jung's II./JG 54 with its mixed bag of 50 Fw 190s and Bf 109s under *Luftflotte* 1 to guard the sectors further to the north, I./JG 54, together with I., III. and IV./JG 51 (140 Fw 190s in all, 88 serviceable) gathered along the northern flank of the salient as the fighter component of *Luftflotte* 6, the Air Fleet tasked with supporting Generaloberst Walter Model's 9th Army. Moreover, Fw 190Fs from I. and III./SchlG 1 were active on the southern front of the Kursk bulge.

The main aim of *Zitadelle* was to forestall the next Soviet offensive and, if possible, disrupt – or at least delay – the enemy's plans for further advances. In the six months since the successful defence of Stalingrad, the Soviets had recaptured vast areas of lost territory, particularly in the southern and central sectors, where the Red Army had stormed back across the Don and Donets rivers. But the rate of advance was not uniform, and around Kursk, close to the boundary of the two sectors, a salient had developed that thrust like a clenched fist 100 miles into the German frontline.

The aim of *Zitadelle* was to eliminate this salient, together with Red Army formations massed in and around it, by launching coordinated attacks against both its northern and southern flanks. The resulting clash of armour (2,700 panzers versus 3,600 Soviet tanks) has gone down in military history as the world's greatest tank battle. It was also the

last time that the Luftwaffe would appear en masse against the Red Army. All other areas of the line were stripped to the bone until 70 per cent of the Luftwaffe strength in the east – 2,100+ aircraft – was concentrated on either side of the Kursk salient, those to the north controlled by *Luftflotte* 6 and those in the south by *Luftflotte* 4.

Hitler placed great faith in new heavy tanks and aircraft (including Fw 190 fighter and fighter-bomber variants) that were making their combat debuts in large numbers during *Zitadelle*. In a message to the troops, he announced that victory at Kursk would stun the world, and that the future of the war, and its outcome, depended on it.

Soviet troops defending the Central and Voronezh Fronts heavily outnumbered their German counterparts, while in the air, 2nd, 16th and 17th Air Armies shared 2,900 aircraft between them.

The most important campaign of 1943 began at dawn on 5 July when the Germans put no fewer than 700 tanks into battle, with the support of principal forces from *Luftflotten* 4 and 6. The first morning of the offensive was occupied in providing bomber and Ju 87 escort, and it was not until the afternoon that the first serious clashes with Soviet fighters took place. Having exchanged their Fw 190A-3s for newer A-4s and -5s just prior to *Zitadelle*, the pilots of JG 51 managed to wrest local air superiority from the Russians for the first few days of the assault. Typically, the fighter *Gruppen* would send formations of 30–40 aircraft aloft in order to keep the VVS-KA Il-2s and Pe-2s away from German armour as the latter advanced towards Kursk.

The Fw 190 pilots were also kept busy escorting Ju 88s and He 111s as they targeted specific Soviet divisions in key areas along the frontline. These strikes often proved deadly, with entire divisions being all but wiped out at the height of the German attack in the early days of the offensive. However, the sheer depth of the Soviet defensive positions eventually slowed down the Wehrmacht's advance, and German units also started to accrue serious losses. A similar thing happened in the air.

On 5 July, 16th Air Army (VA) under Gen S. I. Rudenko lost 98 aircraft primarily in aerial battles with Fw 190s. 286th IAD, which had three regiments equipped with La-5s, lost 33 Lavochkin fighters between 5 and 9 July. These disastrous losses could be blamed on poor training, for many of the newer pilots in the division had not flown the La-5 in combat before, as well as the failure of more experienced regimental commanders to correctly direct their fighter assets in the air from the ground. Senior officers in 16th VA also failed to change the tactics employed by their fighter regiments in response to the enemy's targeting of Soviet bombers in considerable strength.

These newly delivered Fw 190F-2s were issued to I./SchlG 1 in Kharkov in early 1943 as part of the unit's protracted conversion onto the Focke-Wulf fighter-bomber. The *Gruppe's* distinctive black triangle markings were soon abandoned after they attracted too much attention from VVS-KA fighters, these being replaced with Jagdwaffe-style markings.

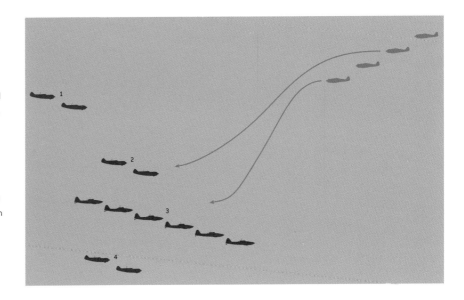

In a typical engagement fought out over the Eastern Front from late 1942 through to May 1945, a formation of four Fw 190s attempt to engage six Il-2s (3), escorted by a similar number of La-5s, from above. The trailing pair of Fw 190s would target Formations 1 and 2, thus leaving the remaining two Focke-Wulf fighters to attack the Il-2s before they too were intercepted by La-5 Formation 4. Should the Soviet fighters succeed in repelling these attacks, the German pilots would endeavour to escape by using the superior speed of their Fw 190s in a dive.

The Battle of Kursk lasted for a full 50 days, and losses on both sides were huge. More than 3,500 VVS-KA aircraft were lost on all fronts in July–August 1943, 500 of which were La-5s. During the same period the Luftwaffe lost 2,419 aircraft on the Eastern Front, 432 of them Fw 190s (both A- and F-models).

As the Wehrmacht had found on the ground, the Jagdwaffe's *Zitadelle* attrition steadily began to climb as the battle continued. JG 51 was to lose five pilots during the first five days of the offensive, but on 10 July events took a more ominous and alarming turn. Aerial opposition was hardening, with Russian bomber attacks on the increase and their fighters beginning, for the first time, to mount their own version of the 'Freie Jagd' (free hunt) sweep over German-held territory.

On the ground, the Soviet counter-offensive was launched north of Orel, smashing into 9th Army's rear. The strength of resistance was now being reflected in JG 51's losses. By 17 July, when the German assault was broken off, ten more pilots had gone down. Present in only single *Gruppe* strength, JG 54's Kursk casualties were commensurately lighter. But on the second day of the action I./JG 54 also suffered the loss of its *Gruppenkommandeur*. At least five more pilots were lost at Kursk. But it was in the immediate aftermath of *Zitadelle* that the most grievous losses of all were sustained, among them a number of highly experienced formation leaders, and aces.

Still concentrated along the northern flank of the dwindling salient, JG 51's three *Gruppen* also continued to suffer attrition in the days and weeks that followed the abandonment of the offensive. Lying in the very path of the Soviet counter-attack, their losses were not just restricted to pilots – an increasing number of groundcrew were being killed by Russian bomber and Il-2 raids on airfields in and around Orel.

But for the Jagdwaffe the real repercussions of the failure at Kursk were far wider reaching than individual unit losses, as swingeing as these had been. Although the initial Soviet counter-thrust had been halted at great cost just short of Orel, the respite was short-lived. No fewer than 61 Soviet armies lay coiled behind their frontline, and in August Stalin unleashed them in a series of smashing blows. To the north of Kursk the

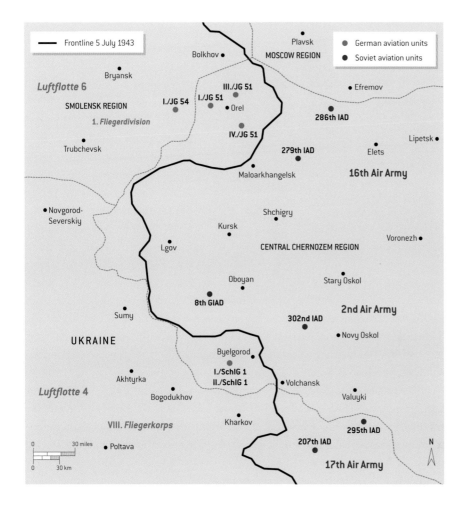

Frontline 5 July 1943

German aviation units
Soviet aviation units

Plavsk
Bolkhov
MOSCOW REGION
Bryansk
**Luftflotte 6**
Efremov
III./JG 51
I./JG 51
SMOLENSK REGION
I./JG 54
Orel
286th IAD
*1. Fliegerdivision*
Lipetsk
IV./JG 51
Trubchevsk
279th IAD
Elets
Maloarkhangelsk
**16th Air Army**
Novgorod-
Severskiy
Shchigry
Kursk
Voronezh
Lgov
CENTRAL CHERNOZEM REGION
Oboyan
Stary Oskol
8th GIAD
**2nd Air Army**
Sumy
302nd IAD
Novy Oskol
**UKRAINE**
Byelgorod
Akhtyrka
I./SchIG 1
II./SchIG 1
Volchansk
**Luftflotte 4**
Bogodukhov
Valuyki
VIII. *Fliegerkorps*
Kharkov
295th IAD
0    30 miles
Poltava
207th IAD
0    30 km
N
**17th Air Army**

This map shows the disposition of VVS-KA and Luftwaffe fighter units in the central region on the day the Battle of Kursk (known as Operation *Zitadelle* to the Germans) commenced. In the six months since the successful defence of Stalingrad, the Soviets had recaptured vast areas of lost territory, particularly in the southern and central sectors, where the Red Army had stormed back across the Don and Donets rivers. But the rate of the Soviet advance was not uniform, and around Kursk, close to the boundary of the two sectors, a large salient had developed which thrust like a huge clenched fist for some 100 miles deep into the German frontline. *Zitadelle* was intended to eliminate this salient, together with Red Army formations – including an estimated 14 armoured corps – that were massed within and around it.

offensive was renewed not just against Orel, but now also against Yelnya, Smolensk and Velizh as well. To the south Kharkov and Poltava were threatened, while further south still, Stalino and the entire Ukraine too. Only the 12 armies opposite the Northern Sector still remained relatively dormant. And this time the Soviet offensives would not be halted, not by the Germans, not by the weather. Maintaining their pressure throughout the winter, they would continue until the spring of 1944.

This entire eight-month period was one of unparalleled movement for the Fw 190 *Gruppen* of JGs 51 and 54 as an increasingly hard-pressed General Staff shuffled them around on their operations maps like so many chessmen from one new breach along the endangered 700-mile front to the next. For not only were the Russians growing stronger by the day, the Jagdwaffe's Eastern Front strength was being eroded.

The seven *Jagdgeschwader* that had accompanied the launching of *Barbarossa* two summers earlier had since been reduced to four by the demands of the Mediterranean fronts. Now it was the defence of the Reich that needed shoring up. And the result? The departure of another *Jagdgeschwader*, leaving just three – in theory, one neatly allocated to each of the sectors, North, Central and South – to stand in the way of the greatest advance in military history.

According to the original Russian caption, this somewhat battered Fw 190A-5 conveniently providing a perch for a couple of young goatherds came down near Glukhov, in the Ukraine, in September 1943. The vertical bar aft of the cross denotes that this is a III./JG 51 machine, although the 'White 0' in old-fashioned German script is not exactly regulation!

Nor was it simply in numbers that the defence of Germany took precedence. The reality of US heavy bombers actually parading their might deeper into Reich airspace had focused the collective Berlin mind wonderfully. And the supply of new Fw 190s to the far flung, low priority, reaches of Russia – never good at the best of times – became precarious. The first *Gruppe* to suffer, IV./JG 51, had already perforce reverted to the Bf 109G-6. Others followed.

It was the Fw 190's misfortune to arrive on the Eastern Front at the very moment that the balance of power began to shift slowly, but irrevocably, into the hands of the Soviets. After its reversal at Stalingrad and failure in the Battle of Kursk, the Wehrmacht would be subjected to a succession of counter-offensives – some large, some small – that would force it out of Russia, right across the states of eastern Europe and back into the very heart of Berlin itself. The Fw-190-equipped *Schlachtgruppen* would fight alongside the ground troops every foot of the way. Despite every effort, and significant sacrifice, the sum total of their endeavours was simply to protect the process of withdrawal. The best that can be said, perhaps, is that on many occasions it was only the direct intervention of the *Schlachtflieger* in their Fw 190s that prevented the retreat becoming a rout.

In early November the Red Army committed its forces to a decisive offensive aimed at liberating Kiev. According to figures from the VVS-KA, some 2,276 combat aircraft assigned to four air armies (2nd, 5th, 17th and 8th) were available to support this endeavour. Of this number, 1,253 were fighters, 400 of them La-5s. Opposing the Soviet air forces was *Luftflotte* 4, which, according to VVS-KA intelligence, had 950 aircraft at its disposal, 125 of them fighters. According to German sources, II./JG 54 (34 aircraft) and the *Schlachtgruppen* II./SG 77 (16 aircraft) and I./SG 10 (64 aircraft) flew Fw 190s in the southern sector on 1 November 1943. Further south, Fw 190F-equipped II./SG 2 would see action against La-5s of 4th VA in the Crimea.

Soviet forces liberated Kiev on 6 November, but intense land and aerial battles continued until 23 December. Now firmly in the ascendancy on the Eastern Front, the Red Army fought a series of successful offensives in the first half of 1944, in full possession of the strategic initiative. The first of these came in mid-January when the Northern Sector of the front suddenly exploded into life when the Red Army captured Mga and then lifted the almost 900-day siege of Leningrad. I. and II./JG 54 were hurriedly recalled from the Central and Southern Sectors, respectively. Returning to their old stamping grounds, it quickly became clear that this new northern tide of the Russian advance would prove as impossible to stem as that currently surging across the Ukraine far to the south. In fact, JG 54 soon found itself retracing its steps back through the Baltic states almost as rapidly as its predecessors had advanced across them in 1941.

By February I. *Gruppe* had taken up residence at Wesenberg, in Estonia. It was joined the following month by II./JG 54, which occupied Dorpat and Petschur west of Lakes Peipus and Pleskau. Fortunately it was a time of minimal losses for the *Gruppen*.

On 23 June 1944 the Soviets unleashed their massive Central

Front offensive that would cut off the coastal regions of the Baltic states to the north from the main bodies of the German armies as they were pushed back towards the Reich. This offensive was supported by six air armies and long-range aviation and air defence fighter units that, combined, fielded 8,000+ aircraft. In response, German Army Group Centre had just the 920 aircraft of *Luftflotten* 4 and 6 to protect it.

The Red Army also attacked Finnish forces still occupying the Karelian Isthmus north of Leningrad at this time. In the face of this threat, I./JG 54 vacated Estonia for neighbouring Latvia. II. *Gruppe* also went to Finland as the fighter component of *Gefechtsverband* (Battle Group) Kuhlmey – a mixed-bag formation of Stukas and ground-attack Fw 190s sent to aid the hard-pressed Finns. During their month's sojourn at Immola in northern Karelia II./JG 54 claimed 66 Soviet aircraft destroyed.

A surprise arrival on the Russian Front that same June was a rejuvenated and reinforced IV./JG 54. After earlier retiring through Rumania, this Bf 109 *Gruppe* had withdrawn to Germany to re-equip with Fw 190A-8s and be brought up to full current Defence of the Reich establishment of four *Staffeln* each of 16 aircraft. In one of the first instances of precedence being given to the Eastern Front over home defence requirements, IV./JG 54 was suddenly despatched to the Soviet–Polish border region on 30 June to provide air cover for the retreating ground troops. It would suffer grievously in the ensuing two months before retiring back to the Reich early in September.

Lavochkin fighters bearing the inscription *'Valerii Chkalov Eskadrilya'* served with several VVS-KA regiments, the construction of these machines having been financed by a specially established fund that generated sufficient money to purchase enough La-5/5Fs to equip no fewer than six squadrons. These La-5Fs were assigned to 159th IAP on the Karelian Front in the late summer of 1943.

On 16 June 1944 25 Fw 190A-6s of 4. and 5./JG 54 transferred to Immola, in Finland, as the fighter element of *Gefechtsverband* Kuhlmey following the launching of the Red Army's Karelian Isthmus offensive one week earlier. Here, groundcrew check the engine and tune the radio of 'White 20' while part of the *Gefechtsverband's* main striking force – Ju 87Ds of I./SG 3 – fly overhead in a ragged formation.

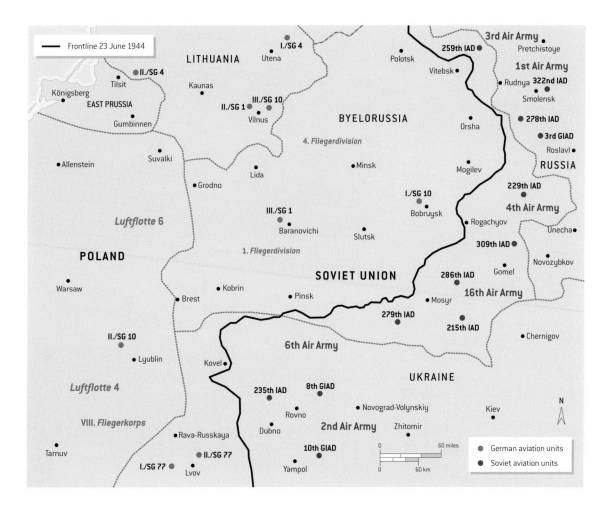

On the map:

Frontline 23 June 1944

I./SG 4 — Utena
II./SG 4 — Tilsit
Königsberg
EAST PRUSSIA
Gumbinnen
Allenstein
Suvalki
II./SG 1 — Vilnus
III./SG 10
Grodno
Lida
LITHUANIA
Polotsk
Vitebsk
259th IAD
3rd Air Army
Pretchistoye
1st Air Army
Rudnya — 322nd IAD
Smolensk
BYELORUSSIA
4. Fliegerdivision
278th IAD
Orsha
3rd GIAD
Roslavl
RUSSIA
Minsk
Mogilev
229th IAD
4th Air Army
I./SG 10
Bobruysk
Rogachyov
Unecha
309th IAD
Novozybkov
Gomel
286th IAD
16th Air Army
Mosyr
III./SG 1
Baranovichi
Slutsk
1. Fliegerdivision
SOVIET UNION
Luftflotte 6
POLAND
Warsaw
Kobrin
Brest
Pinsk
279th IAD
215th IAD
Chernigov
II./SG 10
Lyublin
Kovel
6th Air Army
UKRAINE
Luftflotte 4
235th IAD
8th GIAD
Rovno
Novograd-Volynskiy
Kiev
VIII. Fliegerkorps
Rava-Russkaya
Dubno
2nd Air Army
Zhitomir
Tarnuv
10th GIAD
I./SG 77 — Lvov
II./SG 77
Yampol

0 — 60 miles
0 — 60 km

● German aviation units
● Soviet aviation units

N

On 23 June 1944 the Red Army unleashed its massive Central Front summer offensive that would cut off the coastal regions of the Baltic states to the north from the main bodies of the German armies as they were pushed back towards the borders of the Reich. This offensive was supported by six air armies and long-range aviation and air defence fighter units which, combined, fielded more than 8,000 aircraft. In response, German Army Group Centre had just the 920 combat aircraft of *Luftflotten* 4 and 6 to protect it.

By then the two long-serving Fw 190 *Gruppen*, I. and II./JG 54, had retired deeper into isolated Latvia, occupying bases on the Courland peninsula.

With all but the *Stabsstaffel* of JG 51 having converted back on to the Bf 109 in May, JG 54's two *Gruppen* were now effectively the sole Fw 190 fighter presence on the Eastern Front – albeit already bottled up in Courland. They also now underwent Defence of the Reich style reorganisation, a fourth *Staffel* being added to each *Gruppe*. In theory, this translated into an official total establishment of well over 130 aircraft. The reality, as of mid-October, was that they could muster just 56 serviceable aircraft between them. And a new spectre was also beginning to make itself felt: the increasing scarcity of aviation fuel. With everything having to be ferried in to Courland by air or sea, the fuel situation would soon reach crisis proportions. Before the end teams of oxen would move aircraft to and from dispersals to prevent unnecessary taxiing!

Within weeks of the commencement of the Central Front summer offensive, German Army Group Centre had been routed – 17 divisions and three brigades had been destroyed, with a further 50 divisions missing more than half of their complement. Huge casualties had been inflicted on troops that had been transferred in from the west and other sectors of the Soviet–German front. Throughout this period senior officers in the Wehrmacht complained to the Luftwaffe that the VVS-KA had total control of the skies. This was because JG 54's enforced retirement into Baltic isolation meant that the only Fw 190s on the main Eastern fighting fronts during the latter half of 1944 were ground-attack machines.

Despite a significant increase in numbers (the seven *Schlachtgruppen* of mid-1944 had grown to 12, plus several independent *Staffeln*, by year end), it was still a pitifully small force – some 300 serviceable aircraft in all – to place in the path of the greatest concentration of armour in military history as it erupted through the Vitebsk–Dnieper gap, the traditional 'gateway' for invading armies in, and out of, Russia.

Although their principal targets were the advancing Soviet ground forces, some *Schlacht* pilots still managed to add to their list of aerial kills. The heady days of the Crimea were long past, but II./SG 2, for example, tasked with escorting the Ju 87-equipped components of their parent *Geschwader* during the long retreat back across Rumania and Hungary, continued to take a toll of Russian fighters, including La-5s.

And it was not only the VVS-KA that was inflicting casualties on the *Schlachtflieger*. As 1944 gave way to 1945, and the Germans were pushed steadily back – and the distance between their Eastern and Western Fronts diminished – so the danger posed by marauding USAAF and RAF fighters grew.

Some weeks prior to the final cessation of hostilities, however, the Eastern Front had at long last witnessed an influx of Fw 190 fighter reinforcements. Less than a month after Operation *Bodenplatte* (Baseplate), the ill-advised and costly New Year's Day attack by the Jagdwaffe on Allied-occupied air bases in northwest Europe, elements of some ten *Jagdgeschwader*, including 11 Fw 190-equipped *Gruppen*, began transferring eastwards. In mid-January 1945, with Russian armour already encroaching on German soil and Berlin soon to be directly threatened, fighter reinforcement came to the hard-pressed *Schlacht* units in the east. By then it was too late.

With the Eastern and Western powers drawing ever closer together, and the Reich within weeks of being cut in two by American and Russian forces linking up on the River Elbe, it is arguable whether these latecomers can be classed as true 'Eastern Front' units. Although committed against the Soviets on paper, the majority also had to contend with the marauding Western Allies at their backs.

Ordered to East Prussia on 14 January, for example, I./JG 1 lost some dozen pilots killed or wounded to British fighters, arriving at Jürgenfelde only ten strong. Although claiming several Soviet aircraft destroyed, the unit suffered five more casualties before its withdrawal in early February to retrain on the He 162 Volksjäger. II. *Gruppe's* introduction to Eastern Front conditions was little better. Losing two pilots killed in a clash with Yaks on the day of its arrival, the unit was then forced to blow up ten of its own aircraft in hasty retreats before the week was out.

Equipped with heavily armed and armoured Fw 190A-8/R8s, IV./JG 3 'Udet' was a Defence of the Reich *Sturmgruppe*, a dedicated anti-bomber unit. But it too was rushed eastwards and pressed into service bombing and strafing Soviet forces advancing along the Oder front towards Stettin and Berlin. Although even more impervious to ground fire than the normal A-8, the *'Sturmbock'* was no match for Russian fighters.

Pilots sit and listen to 159th IAP's political officer at an airfield on the Karelian Front in the high summer of 1944. Parked behind them is Pyotr Likholetov's La-5FN 'Silver 15'. This was the 30-victory ace's famous *For Vaska and Zhora* machine, its slogan being partially obscured by a fir tree in the foreground. This titling, which was also applied in silver, appeared on both sides of the fuselage. The inscription commemorated two of Likholetov's flightmates who had been killed during a particularly bloody engagement in March 1942 while the regiment was flying Kittyhawks.

III./JG 11 also returned to the east in late January 1945, this time accompanied by the *Geschwaderstab* and I. *Gruppe* as well. Together they operated primarily along the Oder front and beyond, towards Posen. II./JG 300 was another A-8/R8 *Sturmgruppe* sent to the Eastern Front. Together with elements of JG 301 (a *Geschwader* that also possessed some Fw 190D-9s, plus the only examples of the Ta 152H – the final development of the wartime Focke-Wulf fighter family – known to have entered operational service), it was ordered to the scene of the Russian breakthrough along the Oder on 1 February.

But the danger of having to wage war on two fronts was graphically demonstrated eight days later when the combined *Gruppen* were recalled to combat US bombers over western Germany and lost 11 of their number in the process. By April III./JG 301 was attacking American ground forces along the River Elbe, only to be ordered to about-turn once again. It ended the war in the defence of Berlin.

While the majority of these 'new' Fw 190 *Gruppen* fought over the northern and eastern approaches of Berlin, others were being despatched to the southern sectors. JG 6's destination was lower Silesia. At Görlitz, as part of the *Gefechtsverband* Rudel, its II. *Gruppe* took on the unenviable task formerly performed by II./SG 2 – protecting a handful of obsolete anti-tank Ju 87s of SG 2 that were somehow still flying on a daily basis. *Stab.* and I./JG 6 shared their Reichenberg base with a small tactical reconnaissance unit.

While the newcomers from the west were learning the harsh realities of Eastern Front air warfare, the campaign veterans, JGs 51 and 54, were now both cut off with their backs to the Baltic Sea. By mid-March German forces in East Prussia had been pushed back into two pockets either side of Danzig Bay, one around the state capital Königsberg and the other around Danzig itself. They also held the 'Frische Nehrung', the long spit of land between the two. In mid-March JG 51's *Stabsstaffel* was based at Neutief out along this narrow spit. Once operations from this base became completely untenable, the *Staffel* moved east into the shrinking Königsberg pocket. But its new base, Littausdorf, was soon under constant air attack, and on 28 April the *Stabsstaffel* was disbanded.

Elsewhere, IV./JG 51 had just re-equipped with brand-new Fw 190A-8s, and even a few D-9s, at Garz, further west along the coast. Compared to the painstaking transition from Bf 109 to Fw 190 back in the winter of 1942–43, the *Gruppe's* recent 'conversion' could best be termed rudimentary. A civilian employee from the Focke-Wulf factory explained the cockpit layout to the veteran pilots, described the Fw 190's handling characteristics, warned them never to lift the tail on take-off . . . and that was it! After a few practice flights they were transferred south to the Berlin area. It says something about the men, or the machines – or both – that in three weeks they claimed 115 kills for the loss of just five of their own.

On 29 April Major Heinz Lange was involved in his last dogfight, with four La-7s over Neubrandenburg, but it fell to Oberfeldwebel Alfred Rauch to claim JG 51's final Fw 190 victory of the war on that same date. On 2 May the unit retired to Flensburg and British captivity. For the Fw 190s of JG 51 the war was over.

Which left just *Jagdgeschwader* 54, and it was fighting a private war on the Courland peninsula. But despite – or perhaps because of – their sense of isolation, I. and II./JG 54's scores continued to mount during their final months of conflict. The comparative lull in the ground fighting between each Soviet offensive aimed at seizing the peninsula offered some semblance of a respite for the weary Courland army. But for JG 54's two *Gruppen* there were no such let-ups. The Russian air force attacked the peninsula's supply and evacuation ports without pause. The main harbour in particular, Libau, suffered raid after heavy raid. II./JG 54 based at nearby Libau-Grobin, and I. *Gruppe* some 40 miles inland at Schrunden, took a steady toll of the attackers. When not defending the supply ports, they were protecting the ships themselves as they ran the gauntlet of Soviet air and sea attack. They also provided fighter escort for Courland's few 'Mausis' – lumbering Ju 52/3ms, each with a large dural hoop beneath fuselage and wings – as they swept the sea approaches to the peninsula for enemy mines.

The pressure never eased. On 24 January 1945 the Russians launched their fourth offensive; on 20 February their fifth. The following month, on 18 March, the sixth and final Soviet onslaught began. Once more it was blunted and stopped. But when Adolf Hitler – the one man at whose insistence the Courland peninsula had been held for all these months – committed suicide in Berlin on 30 April, there died with him all thoughts of using the 'fortress' of Courland as the jumping-off point for a last-minute counter-attack.

The capitulation of Germany, and the surrender of all her armed forces, was only days away. For the Luftwaffe units in Courland this meant one thing: escape to the west, taking as many of their comrades with them as they could. The 'Mausis' repaid JG 54's previous services by loading their departing Ju 52/3ms with fighter groundcrew in addition to their own. The Fw 190 pilots also helped their own. Some 50 aircraft left Courland, stripped of equipment but packed with up to four occupants. The faces of those who watched one Fw 190 land safely in the west and saw *five* people emerge – two squashed behind the pilot, one from the rear fuselage radio compartment and one from each wing ammunition bay – were, by all accounts, something to behold!

A bulged-canopy Fw 190F-9 from II./SG 2, based in Hungary in January 1945, taxies through snow and slush while armed with an AB 250 missile container. The latter's deadly load consisted of 30 SD 4 anti-personnel bomblets.

43

Ranking Allied ace Maj Ivan Kozhedub (left) is congratulated by fellow pilots from 176th GIAP soon after claiming his 62nd, and last, victory over Berlin on 17 April 1945. Flying an La-7, he had downed two Fw 190s during the mission – Kozhedub had destroyed 11 Focke-Wulfs since swapping his La-5FN for the La-7 in September 1944.

A few 'Green Hearts' made for their home towns. One or two opted for neutral Sweden, less than 200 miles away across the Baltic. But the majority followed orders directing them to fly to British-held Flensburg, or Kiel, in Schleswig-Holstein, where they surrendered.

During the final months of the war in Europe losses among Fw 190 units reached 80–90 per cent (some Soviet aviation units suffered approximately the same loss rate in the summer of 1941). Losses among La-5 and La-7 units for the whole of 1944, by comparison, totalled 1,044 aircraft. Apart from that, a further 760 fighters were written off in operational accidents and 704 due to the exhaustion of their airframe hours. Meanwhile, the Soviet aviation industry delivered 4,286 La-5s in 1944 (85 per cent of them fitted with ASh-82FN engines, and the rest with ASh-82Fs), and 1,044 La-7s. Therefore, losses of Lavochkin aircraft during this period did not exceed 50 per cent of the total number of aircraft manufactured.

On 12 January 1945, when the Red Army launched the first in its final series of offensives that would culminate in the bloody Battle of Berlin, its armies were supported by 6,719 aircraft divided between 17 Air Corps and eight individual auxiliary air divisions. Amongst this number were 517 La-5s (479 serviceable) and 227 La-7s (189 serviceable).

As previously noted, the Fw 190 *Schlacht* units were kept busy trying to slow down the advance of the Red Army as it closed on Berlin. Indeed, according to VVS-KA records, 13,950 sorties were noted by the 1st Byelorussian Front alone in the first ten days of February, and most of these were made by Fw 190 attack aircraft. During battles with Soviet fighters that month the Luftwaffe endured exceptionally high loss rates, with 25–30 Fw 190s being downed on a number of days. In March, in the wake of these unsustainable losses, Luftwaffe activity in the east reduced by almost half in comparison with the previous month. An acute shortage of fuel and pilots with experience were taking their toll.

Realising that the loss of Berlin to the Red Army would signal the end of the Third Reich, the German military leadership ordered the Luftwaffe to concentrate the bulk of its remaining combat aviation – around 2,000 aircraft – in a ring around the capital in April 1945. They were opposed by 7,500 Soviet aircraft split across four air armies.

On the morning of 25 April forces from the 1st Byelorussian and 1st Ukrainian Fronts met up to the southwest of Berlin, thus completing the encirclement of the city. Later that day forces from the Soviet 5th Guards Army made contact with units from the American 1st Army advancing from the west in the Torgau region. Soon, the battle for the Reichstag began, but on 2 May the enemy's resistance in Berlin collapsed.

During the battle for the city the Luftwaffe had lost some 4,500 aircraft, many of them Fw 190s. On 8 May 1945 the German High Command signed the act of unconditional surrender.

# THE COMBATANTS

## SOVIET PILOT TRAINING

On the eve of the Great Patriotic War, aircrew training in the Red Army Air Force was carried out by 29 initial training schools, 21 fighter pilot and 22 bomber pilot schools and 12 bomb-aimer (navigator) schools. Konotop Aviation College, the officers' training courses at Lipetsk and the Military Academy of Commanders and Navigators (open to pilots of squadron commander rank and above) instructed flight, squadron and regimental commanders, respectively.

Up until the autumn of 1940, the selection of candidates to become pilots was made from volunteers who met the selection criteria pertaining to their levels of health, education and political training. All candidates had to first complete a course at either the Osoaviakhim Flying Club or a Special Air Force School. From 1940 the Flying Clubs would only accept recruits that had completed at least nine years of education at the highest possible level, as confirmed by a recommendation from the candidate's school.

The programme taught by the Flying Club assumed two forms of study for students – either in parallel with tertiary studies (or work) or 'day release training'. Pupils could expect to spend a year completing the Flying Club course. La-5 pilot Yakov Boreyko commenced lessons at the Flying Club whilst in his ninth year of studies at secondary school:

> Following the entrance exams, all of your free time was devoted to practical flying. Your aim was to fly the U-2 biplane solo, and to achieve this the flying training course dictated that you complete 18-20 hours in the air with an instructor. On 15 June 1940, after ten introductory and two check flights with the head of the Flying Club, a bag of sand replaced the instructor in the front cockpit – this maintained the correct centre of gravity

in the U-2 – and I duly made two solo flights in a box-pattern. My flying career began from that moment.

The final exam on flying technique was a serious matter. I was required to complete one simple circuit around the airfield and a second that included some manoeuvring. For the latter I had to make two shallow turns using 30 degrees of bank, two steep turns using 60 degrees of bank, perform an inside loop (which at that time was known as a dead loop), a roll, a combat turn, a spin with an exit in a given direction, a spiral, a side-slip to both sides and a glide. After I had landed my instructor told me that I had successfully completed the exam. By the time I left the Flying Club I had 40 hours in my logbook.

In 1939 the duration of the flying training course at the military pilots' school had been increased to 18 months, during which time students would complete 80 hours of flying on training types and 30 hours in a frontline combat aircraft. Gunnery and altitude training were excluded from the programme, as it was envisaged that the student would learn this immediately upon his arrival in an operational unit.

In 1940 the People's Commissariat for Defence, Marshal S. K. Timoshenko, decreed that the duration of study at the pilots' school be reduced to 12 months. In December of that year he made a decision to radically change the way pilots were trained. Voluntary involvement was abandoned, with flying schools now recruiting students from army draftees. Secondly, graduates would no longer automatically be accorded the ranks of officer upon graduation. Up until then all those completing the pilots' course would be commissioned as junior lieutenants, the chance to become an officer having attracted a large number of volunteers in the peacetime USSR.

Now, a graduate of the flying school would be given the rank of sergeant, and he would have to remain a non-commissioned officer for a period of no less than three years following the conclusion of studies. This move by the Red Army leadership was driven by a desire to increase combat readiness among frontline aviation units and reinforce discipline in their ranks. However, it had the opposite effect as the number of recruits fell sharply and a significant percentage of the students who were enrolled in flying schools were not actually interested in becoming pilots! Finally, discipline in the frontline did not improve either.

To further compound the problem, the winter of 1940–41 was snowy, cold and overly long, thus delaying the onset of spring. Flying training was badly affected, slowing the conversion of aircrew through flying schools. Many of these recruits also found it difficult to come to terms with the new generation of fighter types – MiG-3, Yak-1 and LaGG-3 – then entering service, and in the first days of the German invasion in June 1941 it was these poorly trained pilots who accounted for the lion's share of victories among the Luftwaffe *Experten*.

The venerable Polikarpov U-2 (redesignated the Po-2 in 1944) served as the Soviet Air Force's elementary trainer throughout World War II, some 13,500 examples having been built by June 1941. Praised for its positive longitudinal stability and reluctance to spin, the pedestrian U-2 was the ideal tool for the hundreds of Flying Clubs charged with training pilots for the VVS-KA.

Although the VVS-KA did not experience a shortage of pilots during the first year of the conflict in the east, many aviators were classified as 'horseless' (a Russia peasant who had insufficient money to buy even an impoverished horse was dubbed 'horseless' in the early 20th century) due to a lack of aircraft to replace the thousands destroyed or abandoned during the retreat eastward. Such pilots were sent to auxiliary aviation regiments (ZAPs) and century brigades, and one of the latter was

Groundcrewmen receive training on an M-82F engine at an auxiliary aviary regiment. This particular La-5F had been supplied to the secondline unit after completing its service in the frontline.

deployed to the Arzamas region, where it was intended to train and reform aviation regiments equipped with the LaGG-3 and, subsequently, the La-5.

On 16 October 1942 the new Red Army Air Force commander Gen A. A. Novikov ordered the reintroduction of more advanced training for would-be fighter pilots. In January 1943 the pre-December 1940 order returned, with graduates of military flying schools and aviation colleges becoming junior lieutenants upon the completion of their training course, which was to be of at least nine months duration.

In the first 18 months of the war in the east, Red Army Air Force flying schools and aviation colleges trained more than 40,000 pilots and navigators. The ZAPs also played their part in the training of pilots in World War II. Indeed, in 1941–42, when frontline aviation regiments had trouble replacing their lost aircraft, aircrew were sent to ZAPs to regroup and re-equip. They often converted to new aircraft types whilst here too. Flying school graduates coming into frontline units had limited experience, so the ZAPs tried to give them the chance to accrue up to ten hours of flying time in a combat aircraft. During this time tyro pilots would learn aerial gunnery and how to fly in a two-ship formation or as part of a flight or larger sub-division. Following a month of such training, the aviation regiment, using its previous designation, but with up to 70 per cent of its pilots new to the unit, was sent to the front.

As a rule, new pilots who survived in the frontline for an extended period were promoted to become leaders of two-aircraft formations or larger flights, and the more outstanding among them could even achieve command of a squadron.

From June 1943 the practice of withdrawing entire regiments to the rear to re-equip was stopped. ZAPs now switched to training individual pilots who were flying school graduates. By now the recruitment of pilots from frontline units in the Red Army had also commenced. Separate flying training aviation regiments, staffed by experienced instructors, were also deployed among air armies. It was their job to act as 'entry control', assessing the quality of pilot training and bringing them up to the minimum standard required if deemed necessary.

From early 1944 ZAP graduates were sent to Separate Training Aviation Regiments (OUTAPs), which were tasked with supplying frontline units with pilots that were

# La-7 COCKPIT

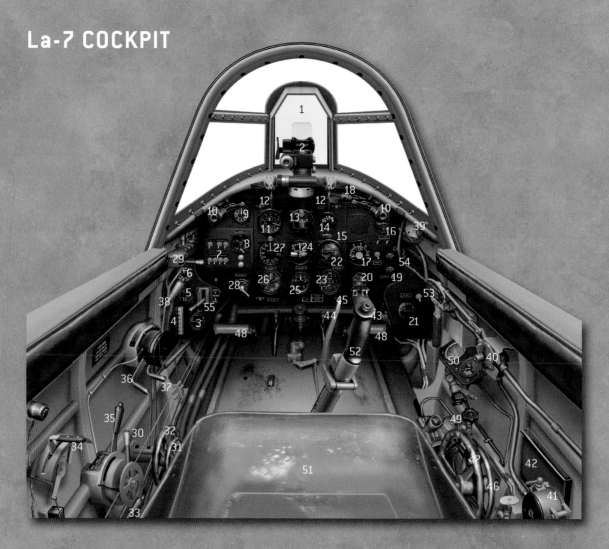

1. Armoured plate windscreen
2. PBP-1B gunsight
3. Hydraulics pressure gauge
4. Landing flaps indicator
5. Brake pressure gauge
6. Air system pressure gauge
7. Electrical switches
8. Landing gear indicator
9. Clock
10. Cannon air charging
11. Altimeter
12. Cannon manual charging handles
13. Compass
14. Course indicator
15. Current reversing switch
16. Amp meter
17. Fuel gauge
18. Cockpit light
19. Radio compass dial
20. Cylinder head temperature gauge
21. Radio frequency switch
22. Vertical speed indicator
23. Combined fuel and oil pressure and oil temperature gauge
24. Turn and bank indicator
25. Tachometer
26. Supercharger boost pressure
27. Airspeed indicator
28. Ignition switch
29. Landing flaps control
30. Oil cooler flap control
31. Rudder trim wheel
32. Elevator trim wheel
33. Manual bomb release handle
34. Cockpit vent control handle
35. Compressor boost control handle
36. Propeller pitch control handle
37. Engine stop handle
38. Throttle
39. Cold start valve
40. Main hydraulic valve
41. Oxygen regulator
42. Map case
43. Electric bomb release button
44. Brake lever
45. Cannon trigger
46. Control wheel for intake louvres
47. Control wheel for fuselage-mounted cooling air exit louvres
48. Rudder pedals
49. Primer and air starter
50. Oxygen pressure gauge
51. Pilot's seat
52. Control column and grip
53. Emergency canopy release handle
54. Cockpit illumination control dial
55. Undercarriage control lever

A typical La-5 formation from late 1943 through to war's end consisted of two pairs of aircraft loosely formed into a four-fighter flight. Mirroring the German 'finger four' formation that had been successfully used by the Jagdwaffe since its creation during the Spanish Civil War, Soviet pilots would either fly at the same altitude or the second pair (the first two La-5s from the left) would position themselves slightly higher or lower than the lead pair.

Soviet fighter regiments would also occasionally employ this six-aircraft formation, particularly during the latter stages of the war. Known as the 'binding four', the pilots in Formation 1 would be the first to engage the enemy. Formation 2, or the 'striking pair', would fly behind the 'binding four' at a higher altitude, the distance between the two formations being dependent on the weather. The latter two fighters would engage enemy aircraft that had evaded the first formation.

thoroughly familiar with the idiosyncrasies of the fighter aircraft type they had been assigned to fly, an understanding of the enemy's tactics and had experience of group flying and aerial gunnery. To achieve this level of preparedness for the frontline, pilot training was extended to one year (including time spent at a ZAP or OUTAP) during the final 18 months of the war. The total number of flying hours for a new pilot

reaching a frontline fighter regiment was more than 100 hours (30–40 hours in a combat aircraft). The time spent by students at academies, aviation colleges and schools had also been significantly increased during this period.

In the opinion of Major Günther Rall, who claimed 271 victories against the VVS-KA flying Bf 109s, in the second half of the war in the east Soviet pilots had 'closed ranks':

Formerly a standard La-5F, this La-5UTI trainer was created by the removal of a fuselage fuel tank and the fitment of a second seat and extra cockpit glazing. Only 28 two-seat Lavochkin fighters were produced by Factory No. 21 at Gorkiy, despite the fact that would-be La-5 pilots often found the aircraft's high landing speed and excessive propeller torque difficult to handle in the early stages of their conversion onto the fighter. However, the VVS-KA desperately needed single-seat La-5 fighters, rather than trainers, so they took priority. The La-7UTI enjoyed more success, with 584 examples being built in 1945–47.

They learned unbelievably quickly. Already by the middle of 1943 their tactics were close to matching those of the Luftwaffe, and modern Yakovlev and Lavochkin fighters started to appear – both powerful, agile aircraft. I tried repeatedly to better different types of La-5s and Yak-9s in horizontal manoeuvres in my Bf 109G, but this proved to be practically impossible, even when the throttle was pushed forward against the stop.

Such comments are borne out by the improving victory-to-loss ratio enjoyed by Soviet fighter regiments from late 1943 through to war's end. During the Battle of Stalingrad in the winter of 1942–43, Soviet units struggled to achieve parity between losses and victories, and this negative ratio remained through the Battle of Kursk. However, by the autumn of 1944 La-5/7 regiments sometimes downed as many as ten German aircraft for every Lavochkin fighter lost to enemy action. By then, of course, the majority of Soviet fighter pilots in the frontline were combat veterans who were masters of their now superior aircraft, while newer pilots were better trained than their German counterparts.

# GERMAN PILOT TRAINING

The training system employed by the Luftwaffe has been detailed in several previous volumes in the Osprey Duel series, so in this book the conversion process that Bf 109-equipped *Gruppen* undertook when transitioning to the Fw 190 has been explained instead.

The first unit to make the switch in the east was I./JG 51 in August 1942. The conversion course itself comprised a series of technical lectures on the handling and flight characteristics of the Fw 190. The most obvious difference between this aircraft and the familiar form of the Bf 109 was the pugnacious size of the powerplant. Ideally suited to the Eastern Front, the BMW 801D possessed two important advantages over the Daimler-Benz fitted to the Bf 109 – its very bulk offered a degree of head-on protection for the pilot, and it could absorb a tremendous amount of damage; qualities that were quickly appreciated in the low-level arena of the Russian Front where ground fire was a constant hazard. Whereas the Bf 109 could be downed if nicked in the cooling system by a single rifle bullet, tales would soon be told of Fw 190s staggering back to base with one or more complete cylinder heads shot away.

One word of warning was sounded, however. If, for any reason, the Focke-Wulf's engine did stop, the advice was to get out – quickly. Powerless, the fighter had 'the gliding characteristics of a brick. As soon as the engine faltered, the nose pointed earthwards, followed by the rest of the airframe in close formation'. Opinions were to vary as to the advisability of trying to land with a dead engine. Some pilots swear they never witnessed a single successful attempt at a deadstick landing. Others claim to have actually done so, with varying degrees of damage to self and aircraft. All are agreed, however, that such action was a course of last resort and not one to be recommended on a regular basis.

Belly landings, on the other hand, offered the pilot a reasonable chance of walking away from the resultant mayhem. The forward momentum of the BMW, ensconced behind its armoured ring, tended to brush aside all but the most immovable of obstacles. The trick, one pilot discovered, was in setting the propeller blades to as fine a pitch as possible immediately prior to impact. As soon as they hit the ground, they bent backwards and doubled as makeshift skis. Some future ground-attack pilots would even profess to being able to make smoother wheels-up landings on their fuselage and wing weapons-racks than they ever did by performing a normal three-pointer!

The width of the undercarriage track also proved a distinct boon to Eastern Front flyers. Where the Bf 109 skittered perilously, the Fw 190 ploughed its way splay-legged and tail-down through the worst surfaces the Soviet winter could throw at it – snow, slush, rain or mud – 'like a bullfrog on water skis'. Taxiing and take-off could, however, pose a problem. Despite the near all-round vision from the cockpit (there was a 15-degree blind spot immediately to the rear occasioned by the pilot's head armour), the large cowling precluded a full forward view until airborne. For unlike the Bf 109, the pilots were told, the Fw 190 had to take-off the same way as it landed: on all three points. Raise the tail too early and there was every danger that the propeller would dig in and flip the aircraft onto its back.

On the subject of flight characteristics, it was tacitly acknowledged that the Fw 190's performance did fall away at altitude. Although this was currently posing a problem on the Channel Front (and was to assume greater proportions in Defence of the Reich operations in the years to come), it played no part in Eastern Front operations where, experience had shown, the Soviets tended to swarm at low-level over the scene of any ground action 'like a plague of gnats at a picnic'. For the Russian Front, therefore,

Pilots from I./JG 54 are introduced to the Fw 190A-4 in late 1942. Note the 'Green Heart' on the cowling and the III. *Gruppe* vertical bar on the fighter's rear fuselage – perhaps this was a machine on loan from JG 51 specifically for use in the familiarisation of pilots from I./JG 54?

When large areas of German-held territory needed to be swept for enemy aircraft, the 'binding four' could be split into pairs (Formations 1 and 2). The 'striking pair' (Formation 3), however, would again fly behind the 'binding four' at a higher altitude.

This is a vertical profile of a typical Fw 190 fighter formation during 1942–43. The bottom 'finger four' formation (1) would have been used to initially engage the enemy, or attract the attention of Soviet fighters, after which the second flight (2) (usually positioned 'up sun') would bounce the enemy formation. Flying above them all would be a pair of 'free hunting' Fw 190s (3), the lead machine usually being flown by the *Staffel's* ranking ace. It was their job to pick off any Soviet aircraft that attempted to flee the fight.

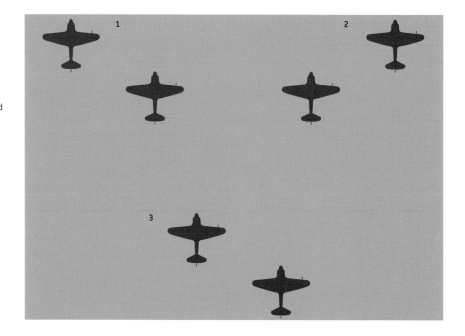

# IVAN KOZHEDUB

The top-scoring Allied ace of World War II and a three-time Hero of the Soviet Union (HSU), Ivan Kozhedub was born on 8 June 1920 in Obrazhievka, in the Sumy region of the Ukraine. Having learned to fly with the Shostkinsk Flying Club pre-war, he joined the Red Army in 1940 and graduated from the Chuguyevsk Military Aviation Pilots' School in February of the following year. Achieving excellent results during his time at the school, Kozhedub was lucky enough to be retained as a flight instructor, thus avoiding the wholesale slaughter of his contemporaries at the hands of the Luftwaffe in the wake of the German invasion in June 1941.

After Kozhedub's repeated requests to join a frontline regiment were turned down due to the urgent need to train replacement pilots, he was finally posted to 240th IAP in November 1942 shortly after it had received La-5s. A sergeant pilot, Kozhedub joined his regiment with 500 flying hours to his name. Despite this flying experience, he had a lot to learn about combat flying and was almost shot down by a Bf 110 on his first mission. Kozhedub finally claimed his first victory (a Ju 87) on 6 July 1943 over the Kursk salient – this was his 40th combat sortie. By now flying the improved La-5F, he had claimed eight victories by month-end. 'During the long, hot July days we literally did not get out of our aircraft', Kozhedub subsequently recalled. 'We did not feel tired, so great was our nervous tension. However, occasionally, fatigue would overwhelm you, and you would have to catch up with your sleep in a nearby dugout between sorties'.

Soon promoted to squadron commander, Kozhedub was awarded his first HSU on 4 February 1944, having completed 146 combat sorties and claimed 26 victories – he was also promoted to captain. In late June Kozhedub was ordered to fly immediately to Moscow, having by then completed 256 sorties and scored 48 victories. There, he was informed that he was being transferred as deputy commander to 176th GIAP, which had just been classified as a 'free hunt' unit. Kozhedub spent August converting from the La-5FN to the La-7, and on the 19th of that month he received his second HSU.

Between 22 September 1944 and 17 April 1945, Kozhedub would increase his tally to 62 victories, 19 of which were Fw 190s – he claimed 13 Focke-Wulf fighters during this period, including a solitary Fw 190D-9. Kozhedub maintained that he had actually downed more than 100 German aircraft, but many remained unconfirmed because they were claimed deep within enemy territory. He also never bothered including group kills within his tally. Kozhedub received his third HSU on 18 August 1945, a feat equalled only by Marshal Georgy Zhukov and fellow ace Aleksandr Pokryshkin.

From March 1951 to February 1952 Kozhedub commanded the MiG-15-equipped 324th IAD in combat over North Korea, although he was forbidden by Stalin himself from undertaking combat missions. Kozhedub continued to fly fighters until 1970, and he retired from active duty in 1978 with the rank of marshal. The greatest Allied ace of World War II passed away on 8 August 1991.

the Fw 190 was to prove the ideal machine, combining ruggedness with manoeuvrability and stability. In short, it was a superb dogfighter – in all but the tightest of horizontal turns – and an excellent gun platform. The Bf 109 could only match the Fw 190A-3's formidable armament of two 7.9mm machine guns and quartet of 20mm cannons by bolting on two performance-sapping underwing gondolas.

The tactic evolved in the west of fighting the Fw 190 in the 'vertical plane' – in other words, a quick diving pass and rapid zoom recovery – rather than of mixing it

The cover illustration for the 1944 publication *Horrido des Jägers Schiessfibel* (*Tally-Ho! A Shooting Primer for Fighter Pilots*), which shows a stylised La-5 being attacked by an Fw 190, was drawn by former *Geschwaderkommodore* of JG 54, Oberstleutnant Hannes Trautloft. This official RLM document (D.(Luft) 5001) was clearly marked 'Not to be taken on operations'...

on the horizontal, was also suited to the east, where the enemy seldom sought the advantage of height and tended to pay scant regard to his rear. In fact, one of the Luftwaffe's major opponents on the Russian Front, the rugged Il-2 ground-attack aircraft, was all but impervious to anything but a stern attack. While bullets bounced harmlessly off its thickly protected underside and flanks, a well-placed burst of fire into the tail unit could often bring about its demise.

If, however, the pilots of I./JG 51 found themselves embroiled in a twist-and-turn dogfight, they were strongly warned of the Fw 190's one basic, and potentially lethal, flaw. In clean configuration the stall was sudden and vicious. Let the speed fall below 127mph and, virtually without warning, the port wing would drop so violently that the Fw 190 all but turned on its back. Pull into a G-stall in a tight turn and it 'would flick over into opposite bank and you had an incipient spin on your hands'.

But a virtue could be made even of this vice, as pilots were told. It was a manoeuvre no pursuer could emulate. 'Be prepared to control the spin, and it is one sure way of shaking Ivan off your tail. Just don't try it at low level. The initial movement eats up too much vertical airspace!'

With this caveat ringing in their ears, the next stage of the course was cockpit familiarisation. There was, as yet, no dual-seat trainer variant of the Fw 190 available, and it was crucial that each pilot be made conversant with his new 'office' before his first flight. Pressing the button high on the fuselage side which released the retractable stirrup step buried aft of the port wing root, the pilot climbed aboard by means of a further spring-loaded handhold and step. Once in the semi-reclining seat, vertically adjustable over a range of some four inches, it was immediately apparent just how much of a quantum leap the Fw 190 represented over the Bf 109.

The basic instrumentation could, of course, be recognised from old, but there was also an impressive array of new electric instruments and indicators, for the Fw 190 was equipped with a revolutionary and ingenious *Kommandogerät* – variously described as an 'early form of computer' or, more basically, a sort of 'brain box' – which relieved the pilot of such mundane tasks as the setting and controlling of the propeller pitch, mixture, boost and rpm. The Fw 190 was also a nest of electrics, which, with the punch of a button, allowed the pilot to lower or retract the undercarriage (a separate electric motor for each gear leg), set the flaps and adjust trim.

All this and more had to be explained, including the arming of the guns. First the fuselage machine guns and wingroot cannons had to be switched to live, then a three-second wait before arming the outer wing cannons – forget that delay in the heat of the moment, it was said, and you risked overloading the battery.

Finally, all was ready. One last check under the watchful gaze of the mechanic standing on the wing alongside the cockpit – shoulder straps, parachute harness, oxygen supply, run a not-yet-quite-practised eye over the still unfamiliar banks of switches and buttons. The mechanic then jumped down off the wing and took station off to the left. 'All clear ahead?' 'All clear ahead'. 'Contact'. The BMW 801 was fired up via an inertia starter, which was energised either by an acc trolley or the aircraft's own battery. A stab at the starter, and the BMW roared into life in a cloud of blue smoke. Twelve degrees of flap at the touch of another button, brakes released and the fighter

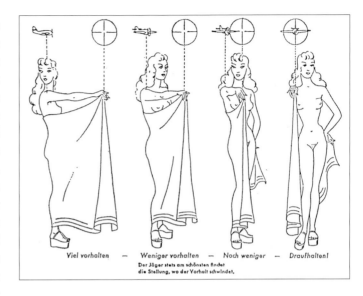

Viel vorhalten — Weniger vorhalten — Noch weniger — Draufhalten!
Der Jäger stets am schönsten findet
die Stellung, wo der Vorhalt schwindet.

... and no wonder if this illustration explaining the principles of 'leading' a target is anything to go by! The drawings are self-explanatory, while the two lines of doggerel below translate roughly as 'The fighter pilot always prefers the direct approach'. What a simple Soviet apparatchik would have made of D.(Luft) 5001 beggars belief!

started to roll. Unstick at 112mph, punch the undercarriage and flap retraction buttons as, one by one, the pilots of I./JG 51 forsook theory and returned to their natural element.

After a few cautious circuits and bumps, they were soon revelling in the superb control harmony of their new mounts, the lightness of the ailerons, the incredibly high rate of roll. Before long, they were practising dummy attacks on one another and staging mock dogfights, during which they found themselves pulling aileron turns that would have wrenched the wings off their old Bf 109s.

The conversion course was at an end. It had been brief, but intensive. For the unit's pilots – the majority of them products of the Luftwaffe's excellent and exhaustive pre- and early-wartime training programmes, and many already veterans of nearly three years of combat flying – there was neither the need, nor the time, to teach them anything more of combat tactics at this late stage.

The transition of Eastern Front fighter *Gruppen* from the Bf 109F to the Fw 190 took place shortly after the early-war pilot conversion system had been abandoned in 1942. Previously, a pilot, upon the successful completion of his formal training programme, would be posted to the subordinate *Ergänzungsgruppe* (replacement wing) of the particular frontline unit he was scheduled to join. Instead of each *Jagdgeschwader* operating what was, in effect, its own personal operational training unit to prepare its newly assigned pilots for frontline combat, henceforth this task would be taken over by the official *Ergänzungsjagdgeschwader* (replacement fighter group), a unit intended to supply the entire fighter arm with combat-ready pilots.

This new EJG was divided into two *Gruppen*, 'Ost' and 'West', and these in turn were composed of a number of *Staffeln*, each of which was responsible for supplying the requirements of a particular *Jagdgeschwader*. Frontline pilots from these *Jagdgeschwader* were rotated back to their specific *Ergänzungsstaffeln* to help prepare the trainees for the conditions they would face when posted to their operational unit.

Although the basic training programmes were gradually curtailed as the war progressed (a result of the growing demand for quick replacements, allied to declining

# Fw 190A-6 COCKPIT

1. FuG 16ZY communication, homing switch and volume control
2. FuG 16ZY receiver fine-tuning dial
3. FuG 16ZY homing range switch
4. FuG 16ZY frequency selector switch
5. Tailplane trim switch
6. Undercarriage and landing flap actuation buttons
7. Undercarriage and landing flap position indicators
8. Throttle
9. Throttle-mounted propeller pitch control thumb switch
10. Tailplane trim indicator
11. Instrument panel lighting dimmer dial
12. Pilot's seat
13. Throttle friction knob
14. Control column
15. Rudder pedals
16. Wing gun firing button
17. Fuel tank selector lever
18. Engine starter brushes withdrawal button
19. Stopcock control lever
20. FuG 25a IFF control panel
21. Undercarriage manual lowering handle
22. Cockpit ventilation knob
23. Altimeter
24. Pitot tube heater light
25. MG 131 'armed' indicator lights
26. Ammunition counters
27. SZKK 4 armament switch and control panel
28. 30mm armoured glass windscreen panels
29. Windscreen spray pipes
30. 50mm armoured glass windscreen
31. Revi 16B reflector gunsight
32. Padded coaming
33. Gunsight padded mounting
34. AFN 2 homing indicator (FuG 16ZY)
35. Ultraviolet lights (port/starboard)
36. Turn and bank indicator

37. Airspeed indicator
38. Tachometer
39. Repeater compass
40. Clock
41. Manifold pressure gauge
42. Ventral stores and manual release handle
43. Fuel and oil pressure gauge
44. Oil temperature gauge
45. Windscreen washer operating lever
46. Fuel warning light
47. Engine ventilation flap control lever
48. Fuel contents gauge
49. Propeller pitch indicator
50. Rear fuel tank switchover light
51. Fuel content warning light (red)
52. Fuel gauge selector switch
53. Propeller switch (automatic-manual)

54. Bomb fusing selector panel and external stores indicator lights
55. Oxygen flow indicator
56. Fresh air intake
57. Oxygen pressure gauge
58. Oxygen flow valve
59. Canopy actuator wheel
60. Canopy jettison lever
61. Circuit breaker panel cover
62. Battery connected light
63. Map holder
64. Operations information card
65. Flare box cover
66. Starter switch
67. Flare box cover plate release latch
68. Fuel pump circuit breaker switches
69. Compass deviation card
70. Circuit breaker panel cover
71. Armament circuit breakers

# WALTER NOWOTNY

One of many Austrians to rise high in the ranks of the wartime Luftwaffe, Walter Nowotny flew almost exclusively against the Russians – indeed, 253 of his 258 victories were VVS-KA aircraft, including an estimated 50 La-5s.

Born on 7 December 1920 in Ceske Velenice/Gmünd on the Czechoslovak/Austrian border, Nowotny joined the Luftwaffe on 1 October 1939. His flying training was completed at *Jagdfliegerschule* 5 at Schwechat, near Vienna, and he was posted to III./JG 54 on 23 February 1941. His first two victories (a pair of I-153s claimed over the Baltic Sea on 19 July) were very nearly his last, as his Bf 109E-7 was in turn shot down by future Russian ace Alexandr Avdeev. Forced to ditch, Nowotny barely survived the following 72 hours in an open dinghy before being washed ashore. By the autumn of 1942 his score had topped the 50 mark, he had been awarded the Knight's Cross and he was *Staffelkapitän* of 1./JG 54.

In December 1942 I./JG 54 swapped its Bf 109Gs for Fw 190A-4s, and it was the arrival of the latter that really allowed Nowotny's career as a fighter ace to take off. In June 1943 he claimed 41 kills, including ten on one day, and in August he was promoted to *Gruppenkommandeur* of I./JG 54. Nowotny celebrated his promotion by scoring 49 victories during this month alone – 21 of these were La-5s.

In September his tally reached 200, and on 14 October 1943 he became the first fighter pilot to pass the 250-victory mark, making him the top-scoring fighter ace of the Luftwaffe at that time. Nowotny was honoured with the Diamonds to the Oak Leaves with Swords for his Knight's Cross.

By then the Nazi propaganda machine had turned Nowotny into a 'superstar', and fearing his loss in action the Luftwaffe High Command removed him from combat duty shortly after he had claimed his 255th victory on 12 November 1943. During the following months his main role was to perform propaganda and morale-boosting duties before, on 1 April 1944, Hauptmann Nowotny was made *Kommodore* of JG 101, an operational fighter-training unit based at Pau in France. Five months later he was put in charge of the experimental Me 262 jet fighter unit *Kommando* Nowotny. On 8 November he engaged a formation of B-24 Liberators and their P-51 Mustang escorts, and after claiming two victories he was almost certainly shot down by another Mustang from the 357th Fighter Group. Pilots from Nowotny's unit, watching from their Achmer base, saw their leader's Me 262 emerge from solid cloud and dive vertically into the ground. Having flown more than 442 missions and claimed 258 victories, Walter Nowotny had been killed in action.

fuel stocks), the *Ergänzungs* system continued. The frontline pilots did what they could with the ever more youthful and sketchily trained material passing through their hands, but the outcome was predictable. In the face of overwhelming enemy strength, many young pilots, however eager and willing, failed to return from their first mission.

Despite the official increase in complement experienced by fighter *Geschwader* in the final months of the war, it also meant that there were more pilots available than there were machines to fly. This problem had plagued the Fw 190 *Gruppen* throughout their time on the Eastern Front, which is why few pilots, other than the higher-ranking formation leaders, had individual aircraft permanently assigned to them. They were simply allocated a machine prior to a mission, the groundcrew adjusted the rudder pedals and seat height accordingly, and off they went.

# COMBAT

By the time the La-5 and Fw 190 met for the first time in combat, over the Karelian Front, in October–November 1942, the Focke-Wulf fighter had seen more than a year of frontline service with the Luftwaffe on the Western Front. This in turn meant that the numerous teething problems usually associated with a new type had by then been pretty much solved. However, the same could not be said for the La-5, the first production examples of which had been urgently rushed to the Stalingrad front to help defend the beleaguered city. Assigned to 287th IAD (as well as 49th IAP on the Western Front), these machines had shown promise but also revealed numerous problems.

As previously noted in this volume, pilots complained that the aircraft was more difficult to fly than a Yak-1 or LaGG-3 due to its heavy weight and poorly balanced control surfaces, although they were impressed with the survivability of the M-82 engine and the protection it offered during frontal attacks. Pilots from 287th IAD also stated that the La-5 was inferior to the Bf 109F and, especially, the new Bf 109G-2 in both speed and vertical manoeuvrability. A report submitted at the time stated, 'We have to engage only in defensive combat actions. The enemy is superior in altitude and, therefore, had a more favourable position from which to attack'.

The fighter's lack of speed was of particular concern, as it barely attained 316mph at low-level and 332mph when at its augmented rating – the latter was only available for short periods due to excessive engine overheating. The poor quality of the early airframes also created excessive drag, which in turn slowed the La-5 down. Furthermore, Soviet pilots traditionally flew with their canopies open, cowling side flaps open and retractable tailwheel extended, all of which shaved a further 25mph off the top speed.

Early encounters with the Fw 190A-3/4s of JGs 51 and 54 revealed that the German fighter had the edge on the La-5, but only just. Soviet pilots reported that the Lavochkin could stay with – but not overtake – an Fw 190 in horizontal flight at low altitude, and their performance was similar when manoeuvring in the same plane. When chasing or evading an Fw 190 in a climb, the La-5 (which was half a ton lighter) enjoyed some advantage. However, its manoeuvrability at speeds in excess of 250mph left a lot to be desired in comparison with the Fw 190. Most pilots felt that the ailerons and elevators were particularly heavy when turning tightly at higher speeds and when exiting a dive. This in turn meant that only physically strong pilots could hope to get the best out of the early La-5s when engaging enemy fighters.

The Fw 190 was also more heavily armed, especially the A-3 variant with its quartet of 20mm cannons and two synchronised 7.9mm machine guns. And even without MG/FF cannons in the wings, the Focke-Wulf still packed more of a punch than the La-5. Whilst Soviet pilots rarely complained about the effectiveness of their weaponry, the two synchronised ShVAK cannons occasionally proved insufficient to knock down well-armoured Fw 190 fighters (not to mention the seemingly invulnerable Fw 190F/G *Schlacht* aircraft). The A-3 could also unleash a weight of fire per second that was almost three times greater than that achievable in the La-5.

However, despite the Fw 190 boasting better firepower and performance than the Lavochkin, the principal advantage enjoyed by the Luftwaffe over the VVS-KA in late 1942 centred on the combat experience of its fighter pilots. The men taking the early Fw 190s into combat on the Eastern Front at this time were, in the main, hardened veterans who had been flying fighters since the beginning of the war in September 1939. Most had been fighting the VVS-KA for more than a year, and many of them had already claimed numerous victories. Their counterparts, on the other hand, had often only just completed their flying training, and all of them were new to the La-5.

A typical Luftwaffe pilot from this period was Hauptmann Heinz Lange, who had scored his first kill in October 1939. A *Staffelkapitän* with I./JG 54 on the Leningrad front from late 1941, he had been given command of 3./JG 51 on 26 October:

I first flew the Fw 190 on 8 November 1942 at Vyazma, in the Soviet Union. I was absolutely thrilled. I flew every fighter version of it employed on the Eastern Front. Because of its smaller fuselage, visibility was somewhat better out of the Bf 109. I believe the Focke-Wulf was more manoeuvrable than the Messerschmitt – although the latter could make a tighter horizontal turn, if you mastered the Fw 190 you could pull a lot of Gs and do just about as well. In terms of control force and feel, the Bf 109 was heavier on the stick. In the Fw 190 aerobatics were a pleasure!

Structurally, it was distinctly superior to the Messerschmitt, especially in dives. The radial engine of the Fw 190A was also more resistant to enemy fire. Firepower, which varied with the particular series, was fairly even in all German fighters. The central cannon of the Messerschmitt was naturally more accurate, but that was really a meaningful advantage only in fighter-versus-fighter combat. The Bf 109's 20mm cannon frequently jammed, especially in hard turns – I lost at least six kills this way.

In the development of our fighter operations, the most significant step was our transition from the closed Kette of three aeroplanes to the four-aeroplane 'finger-fours' Schwarm. This innovation was developed during the Spanish Civil War with considerable help by Werner Mölders. I attribute to this tactic the high number of kills attained by German fighter pilots.

OVERLEAF
On 28 August 1943, Capt Ivan Kozich (who had become an HSU exactly one week earlier) and his wingman Jnr Lt Storozhko of 721st IAP were performing an aerial reconnaissance sweep west of Orel, on the Bryansk Front, in their La-5Fs when they were attacked by eight Fw 190s split into two formations of four aircraft. The Soviet pilots spotted the first group of Focke-Wulfs approaching them from behind at their altitude of 12,000ft, while the second quartet of enemy fighters was off to the right some 2,000ft higher. Kozich immediately turned towards the rear four Fw 190s, which were closer, and fired a burst into the lead aircraft during a head-on attack. His aim was poor, however, so he switched targets to the Fw 190 to the left of the leader. Kozich's rounds hit him and he saw the fighter fall away and crash. By now the second German formation had arrived too, and Kozich throttled back and used the La-5F's unmatched manoeuvrability to perform a tight diving turn that placed him immediately behind all four Fw 190s. Firing from a distance of just 150ft, he quickly downed the Focke-Wulf to the left of the formation leader. Reacting to these losses, the remaining Fw 190 pilots succeeded in downing Storozhko (his demise was credited to Oberleutnant Robert Weiss of 3./JG 54, the La-5 being his 56th of 121 victories) after a period of violent manoeuvring. Kozich made good his escape, however. The Soviet ace survived the war with 16 individual and four shared victories to his name.

Lange eventually became the sixth, and last, *Kommodore* of JG 51, ending the war with 70 kills (including a handful of La-5s), all bar one of which came in the east.

Commenting on the 'free hunt' tactics favoured by the great pilots of this period, 36-victory ace (and HSU recipient) Maj Andrei Baklan of 32nd GIAP remarked:

They would cross the frontline at high altitude in their Fw 190s and then turn around and bounce us from above. The Germans always tried to attack us from the rear

What the well-dressed Fw 190F wore in the depths of winter on the Eastern Front. Heating trolleys and tents were available only for the lucky few! The latter were often reserved for aircraft undergoing in-the-field maintenance, as conditions were usually too bitter in the depths of winter for 'black men' (groundcrew) to work outdoors for any period of time.

while we were still over friendly territory, hoping to catch us off guard. During my four years of fighting the Luftwaffe, I failed to discern any particular pattern to the tactical formations and tactics employed by enemy aces. There was no set form of combat that they followed, hence the fact that they were so dangerous.

With service testing and combat experience having revealed numerous defects with the La-5, Lavochkin set about rectifying these problems with the follow-on La-5F of early 1943. Incorporating aerodynamic improvements, reduced weight (achieved by losing two of the five fuel tanks), reshaped and larger flight controls and a more powerful (and reliable) M-82F engine, the new fighter started to reach frontline units in March 1943. Engine reliability had been of great concern with the original La-5, as the M-82 had a tendency to suffer from spark plug failure and exhaust pipe burn-through. The fighter's boost system had also proven difficult to operate, as had the cowling side flaps – the engine routinely overheated as a result.

With the number of Fw 190s appearing on the Leningrad Front dramatically increasing in January 1943 following the arrival of I. and II./JG 54, it was only a matter of time before the Soviets managed to get their hands on a near-intact example. On the 16th of that month Unteroffizier Helmut Brandt of 2./JG 54 shot the blades of his own propeller when the interruptor mechanism failed while he was strafing enemy vehicles on the Lake Ladoga ice highway. 3rd GIAP-KBF 28-victory ace, and HSU recipient, Capt Igor Kaberov recalled what happened next:

The engine howled, the machine shook and the pilot could do nothing except make a belly landing right beside the road. Of course, the Fascist was taken prisoner. His aircraft was delivered to the Leningrad commander's aerodrome. During the evening of 4 February fighter pilots were brought to the aerodrome to acquaint themselves with the enemy's technical novelties. The prisoner, speaking through an interpreter, gave an explanation. He readily answered our questions concerning the characteristics of the machine.

Excellent it may have been, but invincible the Fw 190 was not. On 16 January 1943 Unteroffizier Helmut Brandt of 2./JG 54 shot the blades of his own propeller when the interruptor mechanism failed while he was strafing enemy vehicles on the Lake Ladoga ice highway. The fighter was quickly retrieved by Soviet troops and restored to airworthiness by the VVS NII KA.

We each in turn sat in the cockpit of the Focke-Wulf and examined the equipment. It must be said the machine was not bad, possessing a high undercarriage and electrically controlled radial engine. Armour-plated glass in front of the gunsight and thick armour behind the back protected the pilot extremely well. But when the hood was closed the field of vision from the cockpit was rather limited.

'It's a high-speed machine', insisted its former master. 'It's not possible to shoot down this aircraft'. 'We'll see about that!' laughed the lads. As time passed, in aerial battles against Fascist aviators, the Soviet pilots demonstrated the vulnerability of the Fw 190.

Although the improved La-5F allowed Soviet pilots to achieve parity with German fighters during the spring of 1943, Lavochkin was fully aware that more still needed to be done. For example, engine reliability was still not what it should have been, with the La-5 suffering a failure rate three times greater than its contemporaries in the VVS-KA at that time. Pilots were also finding the aircraft difficult to recover from inverted spins due to the heaviness of the controls. Indeed, frontline aviators continued to abandon La-5s in an inverted spin until they were shown how to recover the aircraft by Lavochkin test pilots. As previously mentioned, the fighter's handling improved with the advent of the La-5F thanks to the fitment of larger flying surfaces.

The new Lavochkin fighter also had improved survivability due to the installation of self-sealing fuel tanks and an inert gas system, as well as the adoption of central fuel tanks of greater capacity. This in turn meant that the more exposed wing tanks could be removed, thus shortening the vulnerable fuel and oil lines.

31st IAP pilot Leonid 'Lyosha' Maslov (who destroyed six aircraft, four of which were Fw 190s, and shared in nine more victories) saw action in the La-5 on the Southwest Front over Stalingrad in late 1942 and then flew La-5Fs over the Kuban River and Kursk in 1943:

The La-5 and La-5FN were good aircraft, both as fighters and as ground attack machines. In our regiment, division leaders would be equipped with the better performing La-5s, with wingmen having to make do with older and less powerful machines. My aircraft was not as fast as some in my regiment due to the reduced performance of its engine. This was not a big issue, however, as the La-5 was both light and manoeuvrable. Nevertheless, I usually fell behind my flightmates when on operations, much to the annoyance of my

The late-build La-5F was a worthy opponent for Fw 190s of JGs 51 and 54 when flown to its strengths during the second half of 1943. However, the majority of Soviet pilots then in the frontline lacked the necessary combat experience to get the best out of the rapidly improving Lavochkin fighter. This would change in 1944.

flight commander. He would routinely ask me over the radio 'Lyosha, why are you falling behind?', to which I would reply, 'Unfortunately, I'm not riding your horse, sir!'.

When our flight engaged Fw 190s in combat, we would follow our leader into the break and then take the enemy fighters on individually. On one occasion I spotted a Focke-Wulf attempting to flee, so I set off in pursuit. This aircraft was flown by the formation leader, and I soon shot him down. I then saw another Fw 190 fleeing at low-level. I immediately chased after him.

Our division commander told us 'If you can see the rivets, fire'. The gunsight in the La-5 was not very good, so we either fired a trial burst when close enough to our quarry or when we could indeed see 'the rivets'. My foe was heading westward at high speed, and when I got close enough to him I fired a burst. I saw the enemy pilot turning his head in my direction. He then attempted to clip me with his wingtip so as to send me crashing into the forest. I dropped back and opened fire once again, and this time the fighter fell away and crashed into trees. I gained height and headed home. A local artillery battery later confirmed this victory for me.

Three Fw 190A-4s of 5./JG 54 bask in spring sunshine at Siverskaya in the late spring of 1943. Recently freed from their winter white, many II. *Gruppe* aircraft were given a distinctive new camouflage scheme combining what has been described as tan, or brown, with two shades of green. Note that both *Geschwader* and *Gruppe* badges are still being worn, and also black *Staffel* numbers. 'Black 5' was the mount of Austrian Oberleutnant Max Stotz, who became *Staffelkapitän* of 5./JG 54 later that same summer, only to be reported missing in action near Vitebsk on 19 August 1943. All bar 16 of his 189 kills were gained with II. *Gruppe*.

4th GIAK of the Baltic Fleet Air Force also saw plenty of action with the La-5 and La-5F in the early months of 1943, prompting the unit's commanding officer, Capt Vladimir Golubev (subsequently an HSU), to table the following recommendations:

The Fw 190, whilst it has powerful weaponry, seeks head-to-head combat, and the rest of the tactics employed remain the same (using the sun, cloud cover etc.) as when fighting the Me 109. You can only break off combat in a dive. When we first encountered the enemy, we found that we climbed more rapidly in the La-5, and when we gained an advantage in speed the Fw 190 rolled onto its back and dived away. After a few vertical attacks the Focke-Wulf fighters always ended up beneath us. When fighting in the horizontal plane, the La-5 has the better performance in a combat turn, and we were not afraid of engaging an Fw 190 at slow speeds.

If you find an Fw 190 on your tail, never attempt to break away from it by diving. You need to disengage either by climbing or side-slipping. Frontal attacks on the Fw 190 are not to be recommended either, as the aircraft has a small cross-section and is heavily armed. It is best to attack from the rear, as accurate fire from this direction will damage the fighter's fuel tanks. You need to direct your fire at the cockpit and along the right hand side of the fuselage, where the wiring for the fighter's electrical system is located. If this is destroyed the Fw 190 pilot will have to quickly force-land.

By July 1943 the first examples of the definitive La-5FN had started to reach 32nd GIAP just as the Battle of Kursk erupted. Featuring the direct fuel injected 1,850hp M-82FN engine, lowered rear fuselage decking and myriad other changes, the fighter soon made its mark in combat. One of the pilots that took the aircraft into combat at this time was HSU Capt Vladimir Garanin, who noted:

Combats were fought at altitudes up to 13,000ft with obvious advantages over the Fw 190 and Bf 109, both in speed and in horizontal and vertical manoeuvring. The La-5FN with an open canopy overtakes hostile fighters, albeit slowly, gets on their tails during banked turns and in vertical combat always turns to get above the enemy.

The La-5FN was not perfect, however, pilots complaining that their ability to train their guns onto a target was made more difficult by the enlarged air intake atop the cowling. The gunsight was also positioned too high as a result, thus preventing pilots from using it with the canopy shut. The cockpit, which could often be excessively hot due to poor ventilation, was routinely filled with noxious exhaust gases in flight. Finally, the radio fitted to the La-5FN was unreliable at best. Nevertheless, the new fighter proved a handful for the Fw 190, as La-5 ace Vladimir Orekhov (who was credited with 19 and two shared victories, including ten Fw 190s – he claimed four Focke-Wulfs during the Kursk battles) of 32nd GIAP reported in late 1943:

The aircraft as a whole is not bad. It's best not to make a frontal attack on the Fw 190, as it has very powerful weaponry – four cannons. It is very good in a dive and breaks off combat well if the pilot is engaged at medium to high altitude. An experienced Fw 190

Although most sources have linked this famous La-5 (seen here near war's end) with 46-victory ace Georgii Kostylev and his service with 3rd GIAP, he in fact flew only older aircraft whilst with the regiment. In reality, the ace flew this La-5 only after joining 4th GIAP-KBF in late August 1943. Aside from its dramatic mouth, the fighter also boasts a Guards badge beneath the cockpit, which has had the standard banner titling *Gvardiia* (Guards) replaced with the word *Slava* (Glory).

pilot practically never fights in the vertical plane. If you were to compare the Fw 190 to the Me 109G, the 'Messer' would be slightly stronger overall when employed as a fighter, possessing greater speed and better manoeuvrability in a vertical fight.

This viewed was shared by Pavel Boykov of 113th GIAP:

The Fw 190's powerful engine guaranteed high speed, but in combat it could be both heavy and inert. In an effort to offset these disadvantage the fascists created mixed groups. The Focke-Wulfs, as a rule, flew lower, and willingly pressed our fighters in combat head-on, but the Me 109s overhead preferred to dive on us from above and behind.

The Luftwaffe believed that the La-5FN posed the greatest threat to its fighters and bombers from mid-1943, and when an example force landed relatively intact in German-held territory, it was quickly returned to airworthiness. The task of flight-testing the fighter was given to Hans Werner Lerche, who performed his first flight in the La-5FN at the Rechlin test centre in the late summer of 1943. As part of his evaluation, he flew the aircraft against an Fw 190A-8 and a Bf 109G, noting:

The La-5FN represents significant progress in both performance and operational characteristics when compared to early Soviet fighters. Its performance at altitudes up to 3,000m [9,840ft] warrants special attention. However, its maximum speed at any altitude is less than that of German fighters. The fighter's best rate of climb at low level compares favourably with that achieved in the Fw 190A-8 and Bf 109G. The La-5FN's rate of climb and rate of turn at 3,000m [9,840ft] is comparable to the Fw 190A. This is because the efficiency of the fighter's ailerons is truly outstanding. At an air speed of 450km/h [280mph], a roll can be performed in less than four seconds. However, at 600km/h [375mph] pressure on the ailerons becomes excessive. At 1,000m [3,280ft] a maximum rate 360-degree horizontal turn can be performed in 25 seconds using engine boost.

In view of the merits of its engine, the La-5FN is more suited to low altitude combat. Its maximum speed at low level is comparable with that of the Fw 190A-8 and Bf 109G on boost. Acceleration characteristics are balanced. The La-5FN is bettered by the

Bf 109G with MW 50 both in terms of its top speed and rate of climb at any altitude. The Russian fighter is superior to the Fw 190A-8 up to 3,000m [9,840ft].

You should dive in order to escape an attack from a La-5FN.

Lerche emphasised the fact that the La-5FN was slower than its German fighter rivals. However, when a captured Fw 190A-8 was tested against an La-5FN at an altitude of 13,120ft in the USSR in 1944, the opposite appeared to be true! This was not surprising, as the Lavochkin used in the tests was a factory-fresh machine, while the La-5FN test flown by Lerche was almost certainly a combat-weary example.

As Leonid 'Lyosha' Maslov recalled earlier in this chapter, the power output of the M-82FN could vary greatly from engine to engine depending on how they had been used in the frontline. For example, if one had been flown on boost for a very long time without adequate cooling, the engine would expand and overheat. VVS-KA mechanics quickly recognised when this had happened as the heat generated by the engine would blister the paint on the cowling, causing it to peel away. Engines that suffered regular overboosting soon lost power, and they remained in this state even after being overhauled. It is possible that Lerche had tested just such an aircraft. Conversely, captured German fighters had defects too, which explains why the flight performance figures for the various Fw 190As flown at Soviet test centres seemed so poor.

Lerche noted in his report that the La-5FN was highly manoeuvrable in the horizontal plane at medium to low altitudes. German pilots soon learned through bitter experience not to initiate combat turns in an effort to shake off a Lavochkin.

Despite the improved performance of the La-5FN, fighter regiments continued to suffer heavy losses to Fw 190-equipped fighter units on the Eastern Front through to the end of 1943. Most of the high-scoring Luftwaffe aces claimed the majority of their Fw 190 kills during the large-scale battles fought in the summer and autumn of that year, with men such as Walter Nowotny, Otto Kittel and Emil Lang cutting a swathe through Soviet fighter ranks as the latter attempted to defend Il-2 and Pe-2 bombers attacking German frontline positions. Indeed, 5./JG 54's Leutnant Lang was to set a new record on the Eastern Front when, on 3 November, he was credited with the destruction of 17 aircraft in one day during fighting in response to the Soviet offensive to recapture Kiev. Having already claimed 35 La-5s destroyed since 13 July 1943, Lang added three more to his tally during his 3 November haul. *Staffelmate*, and fellow ace, Leutnant Norbert Hannig witnessed the destruction of two of them:

On 14 October 1943, while flying this Fw 190A-6, Hauptmann Walter Nowotny, *Gruppenkommandeur* of I./JG 54, scored his 250th victory, thus making him the Luftwaffe's leading ace of the time. Seen at Vitebsk a short while later, Wk-Nr. 410004 had its standard grey camouflage finish heavily overpainted in two shades of green. Note the small 'white 8' in the angle of the command chevrons (believed to be a reference to an earlier favourite aircraft) and Nowotny's additional 'lucky 13' below the cockpit sill.

The Soviet assault on Kiev commenced with artillery barrages from both north and south, together with a mass of bombers and ground-attack aircraft supported by hordes of La-5 and Yak-7 fighters. Wherever

Leutnant Emil Lang of 5./JG 54 punches the air in celebration after claiming 17 victories on 3 November 1943 to take his tally past the century mark. Standing alongside him is fellow ace Leutnant Norbert Hannig, who watched Lang down two La-5s from the ground.

you looked Soviet aircraft filled the sky, undisturbed by German flak or fighters. They seemed oblivious to the fact that our fighters were operating in the area and scoring successes. In one of the few quiet moments Leutnant Lang took off for his third mission of the day, having already claimed nine victories during two morning patrols. He and his wingman, Unteroffizier Paschke, disappeared off to the west. Wave after wave of Soviet Il-2s were coming in, dropping their bombs on our positions ringing Kiev and then immediately turning back eastwards. The *Shturmoviks*, operating from a forward landing ground on the eastern bank of the river Dniepr, barely 15km [9 miles] away from us, were passing almost directly overhead, wheels down, in unbroken procession.

Sixty minutes after taking off, Lang and Paschke came back in to land. We had been standing in a hangar doorway watching the approach of more Il-2s, and their fighter umbrella, when we spotted our two Fw 190s diving in behind them from the east. Lang closed right in on one of the La-5 escorts, fired a short burst at a range of 50 metres [165ft], banked quickly left, got on the tail of a second Lavochkin fighter and gave it the same treatment. Both aircraft broke up in the air, a wing snapping off one and pieces of another crashing down to the ground near where we stood. Neither pilot stood a chance.

The sheer number of aircraft available to the VVS-KA, most of which were flown by better-trained pilots, eventually carried the day. For example, some 1,500 La-5FNs had been delivered to frontline units by the end of 1943.

In early 1944 most Fw 190 fighter units on the Eastern Front were transferred west to help defend Germany from daylight bombing raids. *Schlachtgruppen* now became the principal Fw 190 operators engaged by Soviet fighter regiments, and these proved to be tricky opponents. Leutnant Fritz Seyffardt served with II./SchlG 1, and he would end the war with 30 victories to his name, a number of which were La-5s:

I flew the Fw 190A, F and G models, and also the Bf 109. The difference between the Fw 190 and the Bf 109 was that there was more room in the Focke-Wulf's cockpit and the controls were simpler – for example, landing flaps and trim were electric. Another pronounced difference was the stability of the Fw 190. Thanks to its through-wing spars and wide landing gear, the machine was far more stable in flight, and especially in landing on rough fields. At higher altitudes, engine performance was inadequate, however.

Normal range of the later F-models was approximately 375–425 miles. The average mission on the Russian Front lasted 45–60 minutes. Firepower was very good. As a rule we had two 20mm cannons and two machine guns. There was also provision for two additional 20mm cannons in the outer wing panels.

As a flying tactic, we had the greatest success when we flew in open formation, in other words with approximately 80 to 100 metres [262 to 328ft] separation between aircraft. In the target area we split into two-plane Rotte elements for the attack, only re-assembling into larger formations on the return flight. During my 500+ missions, I made several belly landings – something that could be easily done in the rugged Fw 190.

With the Fw 190 possessing a superior speed to the La-5FN in a dive, *Schlachtflieger* would usually drop their bombs and then push the noses of their aircraft towards the ground and escape westward at high speed. A report from 322nd IAD illustrated the problem now posed by Focke-Wulf fighter-bombers:

Pilots from an unidentified regiment appear to be listening to a letter being read out by the officer sitting in the centre of the group. Behind them is an La-7 which has been partially parked beneath camouflage netting. This photograph was almost certainly taken in the final weeks of the war.

Fw 190 attack aircraft usually hit targets in groups of six to nine. They release their bombs from a dive, which allows them to accelerate to high speed and depart for their own territory at low level. They don't enter into battle with our fighters, choosing to depart like serpents when they come under attack. Enemy pilots never fight in the vertical plane, where the La-5FN is stronger, preferring to break off combat by rolling away – a tactic long employed by conventional Fw 190 fighters.

Having received numerous complaints from the VVS-KA that its units were having trouble catching Fw 190F/Gs and bomb-toting Fw 190A-8s, Lavochkin responded with the accelerated development of the La-7. Although it was powered by the same ASh-82FN engine as the La-5FN, the La-7 featured numerous aerodynamic improvements and effective weight saving that ultimately boosted its top speed to 373mph at low-level and 425mph at 20,000ft.

The La-7's arrival in the frontline from August 1944 also coincided with the VVS-KA's adoption of 'free hunt' tactics as employed by German fighter units from the start of the war. Special 'free hunt' regiments were specifically formed and equipped with the new fighter, the most effective of these being 176th GIAP. Its pilots were ordered not to engage in long battles with the enemy, but to conduct sudden strikes, using the sun or cloud cover, and then break away from the engagement.

Following the regiment's conversion from the La-5FN to the La-7, its commander, Col P. F. Chupikov, organised effective reconnaissance missions over local Luftwaffe airfields and chaired tactical conferences that saw Soviet fighter tactics compared with those of the enemy. He also made sure that a radio compass (to improve pilot orientation in poor weather conditions) and a combat camera (to confirm aerial victories) were installed in each La-7.

Amongst the aces to see combat in the new type was Capt Nikolay Skomorokhov (who personally destroyed 46 enemy aircraft, including 18 Fw 190s, and was twice a Hero of the Soviet Union) of 164th IAP. A veteran LaGG-3 and La-5/5FN pilot who had been in the frontline since November 1942, he first took the La-7 into action in March 1945:

This tactical formation was adopted by La-7-equipped regiments during the final months of the war in Europe. Dubbed the 'frontline formation', it was employed when searching for increasingly elusive German fighter-bombers (primarily Fw 190s) targeting Red Army positions at low altitude. As enemy aircraft became more and more scarce, La-7 units employed the 'frontline formation' to target German troop columns and panzers, as well as hidden weapons emplacements.

Having initially sat in the cockpit and familiarised myself with the aircraft's idiosyncrasies, I then took off, with Fillipov as my wingman. I performed a few rolls and vertical climbs – this aircraft was a beast! My conversion ended there.

A short while later our ground-based fighter controller directed us to the Kapolnash–Nieka region, where we spotted ten Fw 190s in front of us that were about to attack our troops. There was no time to waste. I immediately despatched an aircraft that was flying on its own and then opened fire on a second machine. This caused panic to set in amongst the surviving Focke-Wulf pilots, who scattered in different directions and raced back home at low altitude. Eight more Fw 190s then appeared, and when they tried to commence a bombing run Fillipov and I again managed to shoot down a fighter apiece.

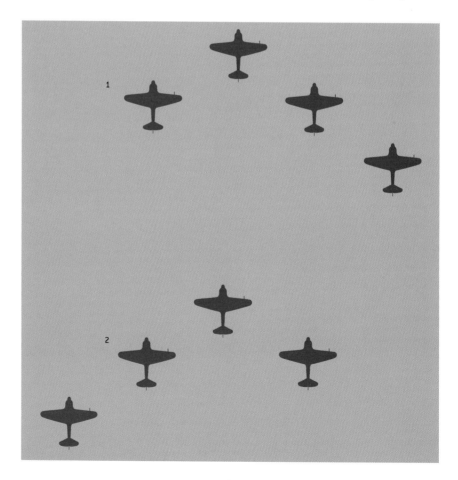

Another formation used by La-7 regiments at war's end saw the lead 'binding four' flight (1) trailed by a second 'striking formation' of four fighters (2), the latter machines being stepped up at a higher altitude.

# ENGAGING THE ENEMY

As this artwork clearly shows, Soviet gunsights were considerably smaller in size than those fitted in German and western Allied fighters. The La-7 was equipped with the new PBP-1B gunsight, which was an improved version of the PBP-1 fitted in the La-5F/FN. Soviet gunsights were strongly influenced by the equipment fitted to Lend-Lease British and American fighters flown by the VVS-KA.

Victory claims made by Soviet pilots were thoroughly scrutinised by both the squadron intelligence officer/adjutant and an officer of the NKVD (political and military police). The process of accreditation for an aerial victory is described here by La-5 ace Capt Vladimir Orekhov of 32nd GIAP.

'After the mission, pilots gathered together and each one would talk about how many aeroplanes they had personally shot down and how many they had observed their comrades shooting down. The squadron adjutant made notes based on these verbal accounts, which he would then compile into an official document known as the "Combat Report of the Fulfilled Mission". Such a document had to be created after every mission, and it contained data detailing the results of the mission, and the pilots who claimed kills. At the end of the day, all such reports were collected and sent to the regimental HQ, where the regiment's combat report was completed.

'Kills were usually confirmed by the commander of the regiment. To get confirmation, one of the following "proofs" had to be available – confirmation from at least two other pilots who took part in the action; confirmation from ground troops; or confirmation from partisans. These forms of verification were equal, but sometimes – especially if the fight took place over enemy territory, or there were other fighters involved – the last two "proofs" were obligatory.'

Having seen the loss of their comrades, the remaining fascist pilots abandoned their attacks and fled.

Fw 190-equipped *Schlacht* and fighter units targeting Red Army units as they closed on Berlin soon came to fear the La-7, for it was the only Soviet machine that could catch fleeing Focke-Wulf fighter-bombers after they had performed their so-called 'surprise pirate raids' on vehicle columns supporting troops in the frontline. Capable of outrunning Yak-3s, Yak-9Us and La-5FNs at low-level thanks to the BMW 801D-2's MW 50 boost, the Fw 190s proved easy pickings for the elite La-7 pilots of the 'free hunt' regiments of the VVS-KA in the final weeks of the war in Europe.

# STATISTICS AND ANALYSIS

Exactly when and where the La-5 and Fw 190 first clashed remains something of a mystery, although it seems likely that the two fighter types met over the Kalinin Front towards the end of October or the beginning of November 1942. As of 19 November, 78 La-5s were concentrated in that very location – they made up 70 per cent of the total number of Soviet fighters fielded by 3rd Air Army regiments on that day. Fw 190A-3s from I./JG 51 were also active in the region during this period.

Capt Nikolay Skomorokhov was 31st IAP's most famous ace, completing a staggering 605 missions and fighting in 143 aerial combats. Claiming 46 individual and eight shared victories (16 of his kills were Fw 190s), Skomorokhov was never wounded in combat and none of his many LaGGs and Lavochkins (he is seen here in an La-5) were ever damaged in action.

159th IAP's Vladimir Serov was yet another famous ace to fly an La-5 inscribed with *'Valerii Chkalov Eskadrilya'* titling. This aircraft was one of 13 identically marked Lavochkin fighters issued to the regiment, which was then in action over the northern Ukraine, in the spring of 1943. Aside from being flown by Vladimir Serov (who was credited with 39 individual and six shared victories – no fewer than 21 of his kills were Fw 190s), these machines were also used by fellow 159th IAP aces Pyotr Likholetov and Ivan Kozhedub.

However, the leading German Fw 190 aces on the Eastern Front did not start claiming La-5s (initially identified as 'LaGG-5s' by Luftwaffe pilots) until January 1943. For example, the highest scoring La-5 killer, Walter Nowotny, downed the first of his estimated 50 Lavochkin fighters on 7 March for his 64th victory. Emil 'Bully' Lang got the first of his 45 La-5s on 13 July, while Otto Kittel, who was credited with 30 Lavochkin fighters, first destroyed a 'LaGG-5' on 24 January 1943. Of the highest-scoring Fw 190 killers, the first to achieve a recorded victory over the Focke-Wulf fighter was Nikolay Skomorokhov of 164th IAP, who received credit for the first of his 16 Fw 190s on 14 June 1943.

The battle for the Kursk Salient in July–August 1943 was the first time that La-5s and Fw 190s met each other in large numbers. At the start of this epic clash there were around 300 Fw 190 fighters and fighter-bombers assigned to units committed to the battle. They were opposed by 500+ La-5s split between three air armies.

Lavochkin losses to all causes (including non-combat) totalled 484 aircraft for July–August, whilst the Luftwaffe had 368 Fw 190s destroyed (again, this number includes operational write-offs) on the Soviet–German front during the same period.

The outcome of aerial battles on the Eastern Front often depended more on the skills of the pilots strapped into the opposing fighters, rather than the technical superiority of their respective machines. This was particularly the case over the Kursk Salient, where veteran German aces at the very zenith of their abilities as fighter pilots fought massed ranks of Lavochkin and Yak fighters manned by young aviators fresh from flying training schools. This in turn meant that during July and August 1943 more than 85 per cent of the La-5 pilots posted as killed or missing in combat were junior lieutenants who had only recently graduated from military flying schools. For example, on 5 July all 12 La-5Fs lost by 286th IAD's 265th and 721st IAPs were flown by junior lieutenants. That day JG 51 claimed 26 LaGG-5s and JG 54 18, whilst many more were credited to Bf 109G-equipped JGs 3 and 52.

Major Horst Ademeit (in cap) took over from Walter Nowotny as *Gruppenkommandeur* of I./JG 54 in February 1944. Like his predecessor, Ademeit had a penchant for shooting down La-5s, claiming at least ten in his final tally of 166 victories. On 7 August 1944 Ademeit, flying an Fw 190A-5, pursued an Il-2 eastward over Soviet lines near Dünaberg and failed to return to base. He remains listed as missing to this day.

Oberleutnant Otto Kittel was JG 54's highest scoring ace, claiming 267 victories (including 31 La-5s) between 24 June 1941 and 14 February 1945. A veteran of 583 missions, Kittel was shot down and killed by return fire from an Il-2 that he was attacking near Dzukste, in the Courland pocket, shortly after claiming his final success.

As noted earlier, despite suffering terrible losses through to the end of 1943, Soviet fighter regiments began to enjoy the upper hand in combat during early 1944 after Fw 190 fighter units were pulled back to defend Germany from USAAF daylight bombing raids. Focke-Wulf fighters remained in-theatre, however, but they were in the main flown by *Schlachtflieger* who were, first and foremost, ground attack pilots. This meant that veteran VVS-KA aviators who had survived the carnage of 1941–43 now began to prevail in the skies over the Eastern Front in their significantly improved La-5FN fighters. 322nd IAD was heavily involved in operations against Fw 190 fighter-bombers in the Vitebsk region at this time, and between 1 October 1943 and 1 March 1944 its pilots claimed 81 German aircraft destroyed, including 52 Focke-Wulfs, for the loss of 26 La-5FNs in aerial combat.

Large-scale battles similar to those fought over Kursk in July 1943 took place once again from 22 June 1944 when the Red Army launched its summer offensive against German forces in the Central Sector. The only fighter units equipped with Fw 190s in the east at this time were I., II. and IV./JG 54 with 121 Fw 190A-8s, although seven *Schlachtgruppen* shared close to 200 Fw 190F/Gs between them. Ranged against them were more than 750 La-5FNs split between four fighter divisions.

Unlike the previous year, when the Lavochkin regiments suffered terrible losses at the hands of the Fw 190 fighter *Gruppen*, this time it was the Focke-Wulf units (principally the *Schlachtgruppen*) that were decimated. JG 54 lost 115 aircraft to all causes in July–August 1944, while the fighter-bomber units lost 498 aircraft. Although a number of these machines were downed by flak or destroyed on the ground in Soviet airfield attacks, many Fw 190s fell victim to marauding La-5FNs. The four fighter divisions lost 76 Lavochkins to all causes in return. In fact, according to VVS-KA records, losses for La-5/7s in combat in 1944 totalled 785 aircraft, of which just 167 were classified as downed in aerial combat.

By early 1945, the Luftwaffe was such a spent force in the east that unserviceability rates posed a greater threat to the effectiveness of Lavochkin units – particularly those equipped with the somewhat temperamental La-7 – than the enemy. For example, as of 1 January 1945, of 97 La-7s in 3rd Air Army, 63 were unserviceable!

## Leading Fw 190 La-5/7 killers

| Ace | La-5/7 kills | Final score | Unit(s) |
| --- | --- | --- | --- |
| Major Walter Nowotny | 49 | 258 | *Stab.* and I./JG 54 |
| Hauptmann Emil Lang | 45 | 173 | I. and II./JG 54 |
| Oberleutnant Otto Kittel | 31 | 267 | I./JG 54 |
| Hauptmann Karl-Heinz Weber | 19 | 136 | III./JG 51 |
| Major Erich Rudorffer | 10+ | 224 | *Stab.* and II./JG 54 |
| Hauptmann Günther Schack | 10+ | 174 | III./JG 51 |
| Major Horst Ademeit | 10+ | 166 | I. and II./JG 54 |
| Hauptmann Robert Weiss | 10 | 121 | I./JG 54 |

As more La-7s reached the frontline and serviceability improved, so the number of victories credited to pilots flying the fighter also grew in the final weeks of the war. Leading aces of the calibre of Ivan Kozhedub, Nikolay Skomorokhov and Aleksandr Kumanichkin were particularly prolific, claiming multiple Fw 190 victories, as both *Schlacht* and fighter units attempted to slow the Red Army advance on Berlin. Fittingly, the last victory claimed by the VVS-KA in World War II fell to La-5FN pilot Capt Konstantin Novikov of 40th GIAP when he downed a lone Fw 190 near Liewarts on 9 May 1945. This was Novikov's 29th success.

A cherished exhibit in the Russian Air Force's Monino Museum, this La-7 was issued new to Ivan Kozhedub when he was transitioning onto the fighter in August 1944. He duly took it with him when he was transferred to 176th GIAP that same month. The fighter arrived in the frontline with solid grey uppersurfaces and light blue undersides, to which regimental red nose and white tail markings were hastily added. Kozhedub initially had 48 victory and two HSU stars marked beneath the cockpit, but by the time Berlin fell his tally of victory stars had increased to 62. A third HSU star would also be added on 18 August 1945.

## Leading La-5/7 Fw 190 killers

| Ace | Fw 190 kills | Final score | Unit(s) |
|---|---|---|---|
| Snr Lt Vladimir Serov | 21 | 39+6sh | 159th IAP |
| Maj Ivan Kozhedub | 19 | 62 | 240th IAP and 176th GIAP |
| Capt Nikolay Skomorokhov | 16 | 46+8sh | 164th and 31st IAPs |
| Capt Nikolay Rudenko | 15 | 26+2sh | 240th IAP and 176th GIAP |
| Capt Kirill Yevstigneyev | 12 | 52+3sh | 240th IAP and 178th GIAP |
| Capt Vasiliy Markov | 11 | 29 | 116th and 148th IAPs |
| Maj Aleksandr Kumanichkin | 10 | 27+2sh | 41st and 176th GIAPs |

# AFTERMATH

Production of the Fw 190 abruptly ended with Germany's unconditional surrender on 8 May 1945. According to records kept by the Luftwaffe, some 21,884 examples had been completed by 31 March, and it is not known how many more were built in the final five weeks of the war.

Airfields across Germany and the remaining countries still occupied by the Wehrmacht were littered with abandoned Fw 190s of all variants that were still

The end on the Central Front. Fw 190 carcasses litter the apron of Berlin's huge Tempelhof airport, which was used throughout the war as a storage and repair facility for all manner of Luftwaffe aircraft.

perfectly serviceable. Soviet forces captured vast quantities of Luftwaffe aircraft, but most of these were simply reduced to scrap in due course. However, the various jet types such as the Me 262, Me 163 and Ar 234 were of great interest to the VVS-KA, as were the Fw 190D-9 and Ta 152 – the ultimate German piston-engined fighters.

Six airworthy Fw 190D-9s were seized at a Focke-Wulf repair and maintenance depot at Marienburg, in East Prussia, by 322nd IAD's La-5FN-equipped 2nd GIAP shortly after VE Day. The regiment reportedly kept one or two for identification training whilst based in Germany post-war. All of these aircraft were re-marked with Soviet national markings, and at least two machines were extensively flight tested by VVS NII KA pilots from the airfield adjacent to Focke-Wulf's Sorau factory in western Poland. Fw 190D-9s were also evaluated at VVS NII KA airfields in the USSR as well.

In 1948–49, photographs published in the official US government publication *Military Review* showed a pair of Fw 190D-9s apparently in service with a Soviet unit stationed at Görden, southwest of Brandenburg. According to the publication the two German fighters remained in the Red Air Force inventory as advanced fighter trainers until late 1949, when one of them was lost in a crash in Latvia.

The veracity of reports that captured examples of the Fw 190D-9 were impressed into the ranks of the VVS-KA in the final weeks of World War II and used against their former owners cannot be verified.

What can be confirmed, via counter-intelligence reports unearthed after the collapse of the USSR in the early 1990s, is that the Soviet leadership tried to enlist the services of Focke-Wulf chief designer Professor Kurt Tank post-war. He was living in the western zone of occupation at the time, and it was hoped that Professor Tank could be persuaded to work for the Scientific Production Organisation in the eastern zone.

In early 1946 a meeting was held between the head of Scientific Production Organisation, I. Olekhnovich, and Professor Tank in a Berlin building occupied by Soviet counterintelligence organisation Smersh. The German expressed an interest in cooperating with the Soviet authorities, and he asked for money to attract other aviation

Six airworthy Fw 190D-9s were seized at Marienburg, in East Prussia, by 322nd IAD's La-5FN-equipped 2nd GIAP shortly after VE Day.

Kurt Tank in the cockpit of an Fw 190. Not only a talented designer, Tank was also a highly competent pilot who very often flew examples of Focke-Wulf aircraft. Nevertheless, he insisted on being regarded as a civilian pilot, even though he was apparently considered to be the chief of the factory defence flight intended to specifically defend the Focke-Wulf plant at Bremen.

specialists who were well known to him. At the next meeting it was agreed by both parties that Professor Tank, who had been give an advance of around 10,000 marks, and eight to ten of his colleagues should come across to the Soviet zone of occupation no later than 20–23 September 1946. However, having received his cash, Professor Tank failed to turn up for further meetings with his Soviet 'employers' in September and October.

There was speculation at the time that the British authorities had made the German a more lucrative offer, but it subsequently became clear that they had in fact turned down his services. In late 1946 Professor Tank left West Germany for Argentina, where he participated in the development of military jet aircraft for the government of Juan Peron. When this programme proved a failure, Professor Tank worked with the Indian government from 1956 on construction of the elegant HF-24 Marut fighter. Production of this machine commenced in November 1967. Professor Kurt Tank returned to West Germany three years later, and subsequently died in 1983.

While the Fw 190 was rendered obsolete following the collapse of the Third Reich, the La-5FN and La-7 continued to see service with the Red Air Force well into the late 1940s. Indeed, both fighter types would play a small part in the war against Japan too, for on 9 August 1945 significant numbers of Lavochkins were being flown by regiments within the 9th Air Army on the 1st Far Eastern Front, the 10th Air Army on the 2nd Far Eastern Front and the 12th Air Army on the Trans-Baikal Front. The handful of engagements fought between Soviet and Japanese aircraft in the final weeks of the war revealed the total superiority of the La-5FN and La-7 over their Japanese Army Air Force counterparts. In fact not a single Soviet fighter was lost in aerial combat, although three La-7s and a single La-5FN fell to Japanese flak.

Although production of the La-5FN ended shortly after the cessation of hostilities in Europe, La-7s would continue to be built until early 1946. By then 5,733 examples had been completed, following on from 10,002 La-5/5F/5FNs. The last La-7s were withdrawn from VVS-KA service in 1947, although the fighter soldiered on with the Czech air force until 1950. By then the improved, all-metal, La-9, armed with four ShVAK 20mm cannons, had entered service. Although based on the La-7, the new machine had a frameless canopy, deeper rear fuselage, larger vertical and horizontal tail surfaces and revised wingtips.

The near identical La-11, which had only three cannons but increased range, replaced the La-9 on the production line after some 1,630 examples of the latter machine had been delivered to the VVS-KA and several Eastern Bloc countries. Seeing action in the Korean War with the North Korean and Chinese air forces, the last examples were finally retired by the latter country during the early 1960s.

The all-metal La-9 of 1946 could trace its lineage to the La-7, the fighter boasting increased range, a frameless canopy, deeper rear fuselage, larger vertical and horizontal tail surfaces, revised wingtips and four ShVAK 20mm cannons.

# FURTHER READING

Aders, G. and W. Held, *Jagdgeschwader 51 'Mölders'* (Stuttgart, 1973)

Caldwell, D., *The JG 26 War Diaries Vols 1 and 2* (London, 1996 and 1998)

Campbell, J. L., *Focke-Wulf Fw 190 in action* (Carrollton, 1975)

Gordon, Y. and D. Khazanov, *Soviet Combat Aircraft of the Second World War Vol. 1* (Leicester, 1998)

Green, W., *Warplanes of the Third Reich* (London, 1970)

Griehl, M. and J. Dressel, *Focke-Wulf Fw 190/Ta 152 – Jaeger, Jagdbomber, Panzerjaeger* (Stuttgart, 1995)

Hannig, N., *Luftwaffe Fighter Ace* (London, 2004)

Kaberov, I., *Swastika in the Gunsight* (Stroud, 1999)

Khazanov, D. G. and V. G. Gorbach, *Aviation in Battle over Orel-Kursk Salient* (Moscow, 2004)

*Kriegstagebuch des Oberkommandos der Wehrmacht 1940–1945. Bd. 3. Teil 1* (Frankfurt am Main, 1963)

Medved, A. N., *Focke-Wulf Fw 190* (Moscow, 1995)

Mellinger, G. *Osprey Aircraft of the Aces 56 – LaGG & Lavochkin Aces of World War 2* (Oxford, 2003)

Mombeek, E., *Defending the Reich (JG 1)* (Norwich, 1992)

Mombeek, E., *Sturmjäger – Zur geschichte des Jagdgeschwaders 4 und der Sturmstaffel. Bd. 1, 2.* (Linkebeek, 1997 and 2000)

Nowarra, H. J., *Focke-Wulf Fw 190 & Ta 152* (Somerset, 1988)

Obermaier, E., *Die Ritterkreuzträger der Luftwaffe. Bd. 1.* (Mainz, 1966)

Polak, T. and C. Shores, *Stalin's Falcons* (London, 1999)

Prien, J., *Rodeike. Jagdgeschwader 1 und 11. Bd. 1–3* (Eutin, 1994 and 1996)

Prien, J., *IV/Jagdgeschwader 3 - Chronik einer Jagdgruppe 1943–1945* (Eutin, 1996)

Scutts, J., *Jagdgeschwader 54* (Shrewsbury, 1992)

Smith, J. R. and A. L. Kay, *German Aircraft of the Second World War* (London, 1972)

Weal, J., *Osprey Aircraft of the Aces 6 – Focke-Wulf Fw 190 Aces of the Russian Front* (London, 1995)

Weal, J., *Osprey Aircraft of the Aces 9 – Focke-Wulf Fw 190 Aces of the Western Front* (London, 1996)

Weal, J., *Osprey Aviation Elite Units 6 – Jagdgeschwader 54 'Grünherz'* (Oxford, 2001)

Weal, J., *Osprey Aviation Elite Units 13 – Luftwaffe Schlachtgruppen* (Oxford, 2003)

Weal, J., *Osprey Aviation Elite Units 22 – Jagdgeschwader 51 'Mölders'* (Oxford, 2006)

# INDEX

References to illustrations are shown in **bold**.